The Argyle of San Antonio

The Argyle of San Antonio

John C. Kerr

Texas A&M University Press
College Station

First edition

This paper meets the requirements of ANSI/NISO Z39.48–1992 (Permanence of Paper).
Binding materials have been chosen for durability.
Manufactured in the United States of America

Library of Congress Cataloging-in-Publication Data

Names: Kerr, John C., author.
Title: The Argyle of San Antonio / John C. Kerr.
Description: First edition. | College Station : Texas A&M University Press, [2019] | Includes bibliographical references and index.
Identifiers: LCCN 2018046042| ISBN 9781623497620 (book/cloth : alk. paper) | ISBN 9781623497637 (e-book)
Subjects: LCSH: Argyle (San Antonio, Tex. : Building) | Mansions—Texas—San Antonio—History. | San Antonio (Tex.)—Buildings, structures, etc. | Architecture—Conservation and restoration—Texas—San Antonio. | Argyle Hotel (San Antonio, Tex.)—History. | Argyle (Club : San Antonio, Tex.)—History. | Texas Biomedical Research Institute.
Classification: LCC F394.S2118 A755 2019 | DDC 976.4/351—dc23 LC record available at https://lccn.loc.gov/2018046042

For Betty Slick Moorman

We have no city except perhaps New Orleans that can vie, in point of the picturesque interest that attaches to odd and antiquated foreignness, with San Antonio. Its jumble of races, costumes, languages and buildings, its religious ruins, holding to an antiquity for us indistinct enough to breed an unaccustomed solemnity; its remote, isolated, outposted situation, and the vague conviction that it is the first of a new class of conquered cities into whose decaying streets our rattling life is to be infused, combine with the heroic touches in its history to enliven and satisfy your traveler's curiosity.

—Frederick Law Olmsted,
A Journey through Texas (1857)

Contents

Introduction 1

Chapter 1. Beginnings 3

Chapter 2. The Civil War Years 17

Chapter 3. The McLane Years 39

Chapter 4. The Argyle Hotel 50

Chapter 5. The Argyle Reborn 72

Chapter 6. The Argyle Today 97

Notes 101

Index 111

The Argyle of San Antonio

The Argyle today. (Texas Biomedical Research Institute, TBRI)

Introduction

The graceful antebellum mansion known as the Argyle has a past as storied and fascinating as the Lone Star State itself. Originally built as the headquarters for a sprawling horse ranch, the Argyle has served as a Confederate arsenal during the Civil War, a wayside inn for travelers to the outlying Hill Country, a dining establishment known for its fine Southern cuisine, and ultimately as an elegant private club that uniquely supports biomedical research. Long thought of as an antebellum Southern mansion, the Argyle's first owner was a Northerner, an outspoken opponent of the Confederacy, the brother of the Union hero of Fort Sumter, and governor of Ohio at the end of the Civil War. In the Argyle's early days, Robert E. Lee was a frequent dinner guest, whereas in later decades General Fred Grant, the son of Ulysses S. Grant, often dined there. In the late nineteenth century the Argyle's owner was an amateur historian of the Texas Revolution who penned a play depicting the fall of the Alamo, written entirely in blank verse. And for the first half of the twentieth century the Argyle was presided over by Alice O'Grady, who imbued the property with its distinctive Southern ambience and reputation for elegant dining.

Over its colorful 150-plus years, the Argyle has both embodied and reflected the changing tides of Texas history, from the early days of San Antonio through the upheavals of secession and the Civil War, the decades of the US Cavalry's wars with the Indians, the emergence of San Antonio as the leading city of Texas, and, in the decades following World War II, the dynamic growth of the city's scientific research community. This history of the Argyle will trace its evolution and profile the fascinating men and women responsible for building and shaping its changing roles as one of the most significant historical sites in Texas.

1

Beginnings

Charles Anderson, the first owner and builder of the Argyle, arrived in San Antonio in 1858 intending to acquire land and raise horses on a grand scale. Anderson must have been struck by the exoticism of San Antonio that so fascinated Frederick Law Olmsted, America's preeminent designer of public spaces,[1] during his travels in Texas in 1856. In the 1850s the city was a remarkably heterogeneous blend of peoples, cultures, and languages, with its Spanish colonial missions dating back to the early eighteenth century and its predominantly Mexican population leavened with an influx of Anglo Southerners, slave and free African Americans, German immigrants, and the growing presence of the US Army. A visitor to Alamo Plaza in 1860 would undoubtedly have observed Mexican Americans in their colorful dress speaking Spanish, prosperous Germans conversing in their native tongue, and in the elegant lobby of the newly opened Menger Hotel, senior army officers mingling with white Southerners.

Charles Anderson came to Texas from Ohio, where he had been a successful lawyer and politician in Dayton and Cincinnati.[2] The likely explanation for Anderson's move was the US Army's urgent need for cavalry mounts in its growing war with the Indians, especially the Comanche. In many respects Anderson was an unlikely figure for this mid-nineteenth-century enterprise on the Texas frontier. He was born in Kentucky on June 1, 1814. His father, Richard Clough Anderson, was a Virginian and a distinguished officer in the Continental Army in the American Revolution who served as aide-de-camp to the Marquis de Lafayette. After the war Colonel Anderson became a surveyor for the Virginia Military District in the Kentucky wilderness, where he built an elaborate sixteen-room home, known as "Soldier's Retreat."[3] Anderson was raised in a large, slave-owning family, with twelve siblings who lived to adulthood, including three older brothers.[4] In 1829 Anderson enrolled in Miami University in Oxford, Ohio. Following graduation, he returned to Louisville to study law and was admitted to the bar in 1835. Anderson thereupon moved to Dayton, Ohio, where he established his law practice.[5]

Shortly after his move to Dayton, Charles Anderson met Eliza Brown, the daughter of a local merchant, whom he married in September 1835. Anderson fathered six children and soon made a name for himself in Ohio politics, elected first as the prosecuting attorney for Montgomery County and then, in 1844, to the Ohio senate as a Whig.[6] Though he served only one term, he was an outspoken champion of granting full civil rights to the state's African Americans, unsuccessfully leading an effort to repeal

Ohio's "Black Laws." Evidently prosperous, after leaving office he traveled for several months in Europe. Upon his return, in 1848, he moved with his large family to Cincinnati, the home of his older brother Larz, who was married to the daughter of Nicholas Longworth, the richest man in town and one of the wealthiest in the United States. With Larz's help, Charles joined the law practice of Rufus King, who was Longworth's personal attorney.[7] Though the firm was successful, he soon returned with his family to Dayton for health reasons. He built an impressive home there and prospered in his profession, but Anderson suffered from chronic asthma and gave up his law practice. Following an unsuccessful effort to obtain an appointment by President Buchanan as an overseas ambassador,[8] in 1858 Anderson conceived the idea of moving to Texas to speculate in land and horse breeding on a large scale. Following an exploratory trip to San Antonio, he moved there with his wife and children in 1859, motivated not only by business opportunity but also by his poor health and desire to escape the Ohio winter.[9]

In the early 1850s San Antonio was in the midst of a major transformation. The catalyst was the Mexican-American War, initiated by President James Polk in the spring of 1846. Until that time San Antonio had been a sleepy outpost for over one hundred years, with a largely Mexican population. The first European settlements in the area dated back to the early eighteenth century with the establishment of five Spanish colonial missions along the banks of the San Antonio River, overseen by Catholic missionaries and intended to convert the native Indians to Christianity.[10] The northernmost of these missions was Mission San Antonio de Valero, or the "Alamo," located in the heart of what today is downtown San Antonio. In addition to the missions, the Spanish colonials built San Fernando Cathedral between 1738 and 1750, approximately one mile west of the Alamo.[11] The city of San Antonio[12] was founded in 1718 and was partially settled by families who emigrated from the Canary Islands (part of Spain). By the 1830s the Mexican residents of San Antonio were joined by an influx of white Southerners (some slave owning) who had obtained the permission of the Mexican government to settle in Texas.[13] Adding to this diverse cultural mix were large numbers of Germans who emigrated to Central Texas beginning in 1848, many seeking to escape the militarism and religious persecution of the Prussian government. Some of the most prosperous and successful German immigrants settled in San Antonio in the 1840s and 1850s, and as late as 1880 it is estimated that approximately one-third of the city's population were German immigrants.[14]

Several months before the outbreak of the Mexican-American War in 1846, 1,400 US Army troops arrived in San Antonio and established a camp near San Pedro Springs on one hundred acres of land donated by the city. When Lieutenant Colonel Robert E. Lee (an officer in the force dispatched to battle the Mexican army) arrived from Port Lavaca in September 1846, he found 3,400 soldiers, including two squadrons of cavalry and a battery of artillery.[15] Throughout the conflict San Antonio served as a marshaling site and logistical center, equipping and training troops on their way to fight in Mexico. By 1847 the war was over, and the army had established the 8th Military Department in San Antonio, which was so crowded that it was divided into two camps, one at Mission Concepción and the other at the headwaters of the San Antonio River. The commanding general, William J. Worth, took over the ruins of the Alamo, which the army repaired and then rented from the Catholic diocese. By 1850 army headquarters had been established at the Vance House on the site of today's Gunter Hotel in downtown San Antonio, where it remained for eleven years until the outbreak of the Civil War.[16] By 1861 the population of San Antonio had grown to eight thousand, surpassing Galveston as the largest city in the state. By then the army's 8th Military Department manned nearly two dozen outposts in a wide arc to the north and northwest of town. The purpose of this large army presence was to wage war against the Comanche and Kiowa, whose violent depredations had victimized the growing number of settlements throughout Central Texas since the 1840s.

It is interesting that Charles Anderson, an educated, prosperous Northern lawyer and politician with decidedly liberal views, would have come to San Antonio in the 1850s to raise horses for the army. Texas had been settled almost entirely by Southerners, many of whom were slave owners who were passionate about the admission of Texas into the United States as a slave state. Though he had been raised in a slave-owning family in Kentucky, it seems plain from Anderson's crusade for black civil rights in the Ohio legislature that he had turned against the institution. Following his arrival in San Antonio, Anderson commenced horse breeding on a large scale several miles north of town, close to the headwaters of the San Antonio River, on what today is the campus of the University of the Incarnate Word. The ranching operation must have been on leased property, which reputedly extended all the way north to Boerne, some twenty-five miles distant, as Anderson did not own any land until 1860. By one account, Anderson's ranch encompassed ninety-nine thousand acres.[17]

On May 10, 1860, Anderson purchased the building site for a large house and ranch headquarters from the city of San Antonio. The deed indicated that the consideration was $2,995 for five lots totaling 128 acres, located

> within the ancient limits of San Antonio situated at the head of the San Antonio River and fronting on Olmos Creek, said five lots [comprising] what was known as the "Arsenal Lot" the same having been donated by the City of San Antonio to the United States Government for an arsenal site and later abandoned by said government and re-conveyed to the City of San Antonio.

Earlier in the 1850s the city of San Antonio had sold the property to the federal government as the site for an army arsenal, which was never built, resulting in the reversion of the land to the city. According to one account, the Arsenal Lot had earlier been the site of a stone clubhouse at the center of a planned township named "Avoca," which had been founded in the 1830s by Irish settlers led by a Mr. William E. Howth.[18] During the early 1840s lots had been platted and sold, streets named, and a few homes evidently constructed. The township was located where the headwaters

Alamo Plaza in the 1840s. (*A Place in Time: A Pictorial View of San Antonio's Past* [San Antonio: Express-News Corp., 1980], Photo 32, Raba Collection)

of the San Antonio River meet Olmos Creek. The site apparently reminded the Irish immigrants of the Vale of Avoca, a beloved destination in County Wicklow, Ireland, at the confluence of two mountain streams, celebrated in verse in "The Meeting of the Waters" by Thomas Moore:

> There is not in the wide world a valley so sweet
> As that vale in whose bosom the bright waters meet;
> Oh! the last rays of feeling and life must depart,
> Ere the bloom of that valley shall fade from my heart . . .
> Sweet vale of Avoca! How calm could I rest
> In thy bosom of shade, with the friends I love best,
> Where the storms that we feel in this cold world should cease,
> And our hearts, like thy waters, be mingled in peace.

But the people of San Antonio were concentrated several miles south of the Avoca township, and by 1850 it had been abandoned in failure. Avoca is listed in the *Texas Almanac* as one of the true ghost towns of Texas.[19]

The original home built by Charles Anderson in 1860 was a two-story, sixty-by-sixty-foot square, raised from the ground, with steps leading up to the front doors. The house's floors and woodwork were built of cypress shipped from New Orleans.[20] Anderson is believed to have raised sturdy cavalry horses. His sorrel stallions were given Old Testament names, including Nebuchadnezzar, Jehoshaphat, and Elijah.[21] Anderson is believed to have entertained lavishly, presumably inviting senior army officers to whom quartermasters would defer in the decision to purchase horses for the large and growing cavalry based in the city and outlying forts. Among Anderson's guests was Robert E. Lee. Lee had returned to Texas in March 1856, when he joined a regiment at Fort Mason, north of Fredericksburg, one of the cavalry outposts engaged in the Indian war. Colonel Albert Sidney Johnston,[22] the regimental commander, sent Lee north to command two cavalry squadrons at Camp Cooper, located in Throckmorton County, northwest of Fort Worth. Lee divided his time over the next five years between Texas and his family home in Virginia. When he was not stationed at some primitive, dusty cavalry fort or army encampment, the genteel Virginian enjoyed the relatively civilized comforts of San Antonio, where in July 1859 he assumed command of the 2nd Cavalry. Lee's offices were in the Vance House, and he boarded at Mrs. Phillips's Hotel on Main Plaza.[23] During that year Lee became a charter member of St. Mark's

Episcopal Church, the construction of which was completed in 1859. Decades later, his son Robert wrote: "The summer months he spent in San Antonio, and while there interested himself with the good people of that town in building an Episcopal church, to which he contributed largely."[24] As the commanding officer of the cavalry, Lee was the frequent dinner guest of Charles Anderson at his impressive country house north of the city.[25] After traveling to Virginia to tend to family affairs following the death of his father-in-law, George Washington Custis (Martha Washington's grandson and the adopted son of George Washington), Lee returned to San Antonio at the beginning of 1860. Besides being entertained by Anderson, he is reported to have patronized the elegant new Menger Hotel, which was also built in 1859.

Following the election of Lincoln as president in November 1860, Texas was in the throes of the secession fever that was sweeping across the South. Considering his background, it is unsurprising that Charles Anderson was an outspoken opponent of secession and a champion of the Union. Thus it was that in early December Anderson appeared at a large rally on Alamo Plaza and delivered a speech urging his fellow Texans to oppose secession. The rally had been organized by the prosecessionists, but Anderson and other staunch Union men got wind of it and were determined to attend and speak out. Before a large crowd, Anderson mounted the platform following a secessionist speaker and delivered a passionate appeal to preserve the Union.[26] By some accounts he was set upon by an angry mob consisting of members of the prosecession Knights of the Golden Circle and briefly detained.[27] In another account he was hustled by friends into the safety of the lobby of the Menger Hotel.[28] In his history of Fort Sam Houston, Eldon Cagle writes that Anderson "would have been mobbed [by the Knights of the Golden Circle] had it not been for an opposing group singing 'Yankee Doodle.'"[29]

Most Texans favored secession, which was approved by an overwhelming majority in the Texas Secession Convention and then in a plebiscite. But many, including Anderson and the state's most renowned citizen, Sam Houston, the first president of the Republic of Texas and sitting governor, were opposed. Houston resigned his office when Texas officially joined the new Confederate States of America, and he spoke with remarkable prescience to an angry prosecession mob:

> Some of you laugh to scorn the idea of bloodshed as the result of Secession. But let me tell you what is coming. Your fathers and husbands, your sons and brothers, will be herded at the point of the bayonet. . . . You may, after the sacrifice of countless millions of treasure and hundreds of thousands of lives, as a bare possibility win Southern independence. But I doubt it.[30]

Another opponent of secession was Robert E. Lee. In a letter to his son Custis in January 1861, Lee wrote: "I can anticipate no greater calamity for the country than the dissolution of the union. . . . I am willing to sacrifice everything but honor for its preservation. . . . Secession is nothing but revolution. If the Union is dissolved, and the Government disrupted, I shall return to my native State and share in the

Portrait of Robert E. Lee in the Argyle's Spanish Room. (Photo of painting owned by TBRI)

miseries of my people, and save in defense will draw my sword on none."[31] Following Texas's vote to secede, Lee received orders to report to Washington without delay. He returned from Fort Mason to San Antonio and was immediately confronted by a group of men calling themselves "Texas Commissioners." When he arrived at army headquarters he learned that General David Twiggs, the commanding officer of the army's Department of Texas, had surrendered the federal forces to a force of armed men. Lee was informed by the secessionists that if he resigned his commission and accepted one in the Confederate Army, he would be free to travel home with his personal belongings. Otherwise he would forfeit them. Lee spurned the offer, saying he would not side "with a bunch of Texas rebels."[32] In his recent biography of Lee, Michael Korda offers the following account of the ensuing events:

> Lee was infuriated, and went immediately to the home of a friend, Charles Anderson, a lawyer and an outspoken Unionist and abolitionist. . . . It speaks volumes for Lee that he was a friend of a man like Anderson, who disagreed vehemently with him, although at this stage, at any rate, he and Anderson were of one mind about the Texas secessionists. Perhaps because he was angry, Lee was franker about his position than he had been with anybody else except his family. "I cannot be moved by the conduct of those people [the Texas Commissioners] from my sense of duty. I still think that my loyalty to Virginia ought to take precedence over that which is due the Federal Government. And so I shall report myself at Washington. If Virginia stands by the Union, so will I. But if she secedes, I will follow my native state with my sword, and if need be with my life." . . . Lee asked Anderson to hold on to his belongings and have them shipped to Arlington, which Anderson agreed to do. That problem solved, Lee set off for home by way of Indianola. . . . He arrived at Arlington on March 1, three days before the inauguration of Abraham Lincoln.[33]

When Texas joined the Confederacy, Charles Anderson resolved to leave behind his enormous ranch and return with his wife and children to Ohio. He remained in San Antonio through the summer of 1861, arranging to sell his large house, horses, and surrounding acreage in September to another Kentuckian by the name of William McLane for the price of $10,000.[34] Anderson then arranged to depart San Antonio with his wife, who was suffering from an attack of malaria, and grown daughters for Matamoros, across the border from Brownsville, Texas, on the Gulf Coast. They traveled in a covered coach, which he had purchased from James Longstreet, a US Army major and future Confederate general.[35] Not far from San Antonio their party was intercepted by a detachment of Confederate cavalry and forced to return to the city. After several days during which they were detained at the Menger Hotel, the Andersons were informed that Eliza and her daughters would be permitted to leave but that Charles would be held as a prisoner of war on the orders of Colonel Ben McCulloch.[36] It was McCulloch, a former Texas Ranger now commissioned as a colonel in the Confederate Army, who had marched on the Federal Arsenal in San Antonio[37] with a force of some 550 men, including 150 members of the Knights of the Golden Circle, to demand the surrender of the Union forces under General Twiggs. By mid-October the Anderson women had made their way to Matamoros, stopping along the way as overnight guests of Richard King and his wife, Henrietta, at the King Ranch.[38] In late October, Charles Anderson managed to escape from his imprisonment and, traveling on horseback, made the long and dangerous journey southwest to Eagle Pass on the Rio Grande, and then across the Sonoran Desert to Monterrey, Mexico.[39] Eliza Anderson had finally sailed with her daughters to Veracruz, where at last they were reunited with Charles in late November. The family traveled by steamship to Havana, and then on December 11, almost three months after they had first attempted to flee from San Antonio, they arrived in New York City.[40] Thus Charles Anderson was forced by the catastrophic events overwhelming the nation to abandon his vast landholdings and the large home that was to become the Argyle.

When Robert E. Lee arrived at his Arlington home, across the Potomac from Washington, it was the first of March and far from clear that Virginia would secede. At that time, the majority sentiment of the Upper South (Virginia, North Carolina, and Maryland) was opposed to secession, and it is doubtful whether the fledgling Confederacy could have survived without the inclusion of Virginia and North Carolina, with their large populations, industry, and substantial agricultural production.[41] In a trial vote by members of the Virginia Convention on April 4, a two-to-one majority opposed secession.[42] The most pressing question for those, North and South, pondering the consequences of secession was what the newly inaugurated President Lincoln would do to protect the federal garrison at Fort Sumter, one of the forts guarding the entrance to the harbor at Charleston, South Carolina. The Union officer in command of Fort Sumter had been sharply criticized for unnecessarily exposing the garrison to the risk of a Confederate bombardment. And that Union officer was none other than Major Robert Anderson, the older brother of Charles Anderson.

2

The Civil War Years

In early April 1861, the people of the United States held their collective breath. While South Carolina, Mississippi, Florida, Alabama, Louisiana, and Texas had seceded, crucially Virginia and North Carolina (as well as Tennessee and Arkansas) had not. The fate of Fort Sumter, and what Lincoln would do if the Confederates seized it by force, would prove to be the decisive factors in whether these states would remain in the Union. Though until April 1861 Robert Anderson had lived in relative obscurity, notwithstanding his successful career in the army, his name would soon be on the lips of virtually every American. At age fifty-five, Anderson was two years older than Robert E. Lee, and he had graduated from West Point in the year Lee had entered it, in 1825.[1] Anderson and Lee had both served with distinction in the Mexican-American War, Anderson in the siege of Veracruz and the Battles of Cerro Gordo, Amazoque, and Molino del Rey, where he was severely wounded.[2] At the time of South Carolina's secession in December 1860,

Anderson was the commanding officer of the US Army garrison at Fort Moultrie on the seacoast at Charleston, South Carolina. A native of Kentucky and former slave owner, he was not opposed to slavery but, like his brother Charles, was deeply committed to the Union. Now amid fire-breathing secessionists, in the winter of 1861 Anderson moved a small detachment of his forces, fewer than one hundred men, from Fort Moultrie to the far more easily defended Fort Sumter in Charleston Harbor. Anderson's move was greeted with effusive praise in Northern papers and denounced in the South. Many viewed the action as foolhardy because he lacked sufficient supplies and ammunition to withstand a prolonged siege, and also as an incitement to war. Mary Chesnut, the celebrated Confederate socialite and diarist whose husband, James, had represented South Carolina as a senator before secession, wrote: "Now it is Fort Sumter—and that ill-advised Anderson. . . . There stands Fort Sumter—en évidence—and thereby hangs peace or war."[3] On April 7, Confederate general P. G. T. Beauregard, commanding the Confederate forces in Charleston, ordered that any efforts to reprovision Fort Sumter be blocked. In response, President Lincoln ordered the US Navy to resupply the fort by sea and dispatched ships from Norfolk. Determined to prevent this, the newly elected president of the Confederate States, Jefferson Davis (himself a graduate of West Point), ordered the Confederate forces under Beauregard to bombard the fort. Ironically, Robert Anderson had been Beauregard's artillery instructor at West Point.[4]

Early on the morning of April 12, the Confederates unloosed a large and sustained cannonade on Fort Sumter.

The bombardment of Fort Sumter was the front-page headline in newspapers across America, with Major Anderson cast in one of the leading roles. The *New York Times,* in the lead column of its April 12 edition, reported:

> The ball is opened. War is inaugurated. The batteries . . . were opened on Fort Sumter at 4 o'clock this morning. . . . It is supposed that Major Anderson is resting his men for the night. Fort Moultrie [now in Confederate hands] began the bombardment by firing two guns. To them Major Anderson replied with three of his barbette guns.

Voicing the exasperation of many, Mary Chesnut wrote:

> Why did that green goose Anderson go into Fort Sumter? Then everything began to go wrong. Now they have intercepted a letter from him, urging them to let him surrender. He paints the horrors likely to ensue if they will not. He ought to have thought of all that before he put his head in the hole.[5]

Americans North and South followed the fate of Fort Sumter with bated breath. The front page of the April 15 edition of the *New York Times* carried the bold headline "Fort Sumter Fallen: Major Anderson and His Men Coming to New York." The *Times* reported: "Major Anderson has surrendered, after hard fighting. Major Anderson stated that he surrendered his sword to General Beauregard [who] said he would not receive it from so brave a man. He says Major Anderson made a staunch fight." Robert Anderson was now a household name across the United States and the fledgling Confederate States of America. Secretary of War Stanton addressed a note to him, expressing "perfect satisfaction with the manner in which he had defended the post under his command."[6] By mid-May Anderson had been promoted to the rank of brigadier general. He made his way to New York City, where he was greeted as a hero, the first in the North in the Civil War. *Harper's Magazine* reported that in New York Anderson "was welcomed with distinguished honor."[7] He brought with him the tattered thirty-three-star American flag from Fort Sumter and participated in a patriotic rally at Union Square reported to be the largest public gathering in the country's history.

Abraham Lincoln's response to the news of the fall of Fort Sumter was both swift and calamitous. On the fifteenth of April (Anderson had surrendered on the fourteenth), Lincoln issued a proclamation calling for seventy-five thousand volunteers to subdue the Southern rebellion, beginning with retaking the federal forts and other properties wrongly seized by the secessionists. Even more troubling, the call for volunteers assigned quotas to each state (other than those that had seceded), including the slave-owning states that until that point had resisted the calls to join their Southern brethren in the new Confederacy. The executives of these states (except for Maryland) reacted to Lincoln's proclamation with outrage. The governor of North Carolina, for example, stated that "I regard the levy of troops . . . for the purpose of subjugating the States of the South as . . . a usurpation of power. I can be no party to this wicked violation of the laws of the country." Similar expressions of

Major Robert Anderson and his fellow officers at Fort Sumter.
(*Harper's Weekly*, April 27, 1861)

defiance to Lincoln's proclamation were promptly issued by the governors of Missouri, Kentucky, Tennessee, and Virginia, whose chief executive stated that "your [Lincoln's] object is to subjugate the Southern States, and a requisition [of troops] made upon me for such an object . . . in my judgment, not within the purview of the Constitution . . . will not be complied with."[8]

Any hope that internecine war could be avoided vanished with Lincoln's call to arms. In the opinion of this writer, it is apparent that following the Confederate attack on Fort Sumter Lincoln was determined to wage war on the rebellious states whether or not the states of the Upper South remained loyal to the Union. The fall of Sumter and issuance of Lincoln's proclamation occurred when Virginia was in the midst of the state's Convention to consider secession. Pro-Union sentiment disappeared virtually overnight, and on April 17 the Convention overwhelmingly adopted a resolution in favor of secession. Robert E. Lee, in Washington, observed the unfolding events with growing dismay. On the morning following the vote of the Virginia Convention (which had not yet been publicly reported), he received a note from Winfield Scott, general in chief of the army, requesting Lee to call on him. He also received a message from Francis Blair, who likewise wished to see Lee. The next day Lee called on Blair at his mansion opposite the White House.[9] Blair was a conspicuous and highly influential political figure from St. Louis and the father of Montgomery Blair, who served in Lincoln's cabinet as postmaster general. Though no record was made of their private meeting, it is widely believed that Blair's purpose was to convey a message on behalf of Lincoln offering Lee command of the new federal army with the rank of major general. Lee was undoubtedly taken aback by this astonishing proposition. In Michael Korda's version of the incident:

> Blair spoke at great length, and no doubt with persuasive effect, but Lee stuck to his guns. "I declined the offer he made me to take command of the army that was to be brought into the field," he wrote much later, "stating as clearly as candidly and as courteously as I could, that though opposed to secession and deprecating war, I could take no part in an invasion of the Southern States."[10]

Lee departed from Blair House for his scheduled appointment with General Scott. It seems certain that by this time Lee had already made up his mind to resign his commission from the army he had served his entire adult life, though news of Virginia's decision to secede had not been made public. It also seems certain that General Scott understood and fully expected Lee's resignation. Both of their attitudes would have been consistent with the belief that Lincoln was determined to launch an armed invasion of the rebellious Southern states no matter whether Virginia and North Carolina remained loyal to the Union or seceded. General Scott reportedly informed Lee: "If you purpose to resign, it is proper that you should do so at once; your present attitude is equivocal."[11] Lee returned to his home in Arlington, where the following day the news of Virginia's secession was in the Alexandria newspaper. Torn by his loyalties to both the United States and Virginia, with a heavy heart he composed a brief letter of resignation to the secretary of war. Lee then wrote to General Scott, expressing his gratitude for the older man's many years of friendship and generosity, stating:

> I shall carry to the grave the most grateful recollections of your kind consideration, and your name and fame shall always be dear to me.
>
> Save in the defense of my native State, I never desire again to draw my sword.[12]

Having tendered his resignation, Lee now found himself, for the first time since graduating from West Point, in the position of a civilian. In letters to his sister Anne (who remained loyal to the Union) and brother Smith penned on the same day, Lee used a formulation almost identical to that in his letter to General Scott. To Anne: "Save in defense of my native State . . . I hope I may never be called on to draw my sword." And to Smith: "Save in defense of my native State, I have no desire ever again to draw my sword."[13] On April 17 the Virginia Secession Convention voted in favor of secession, a decision ratified by the voters on May 23 (the North Carolina Secession Convention voted unanimously for secession on May 20). Within months Lincoln's army was on Virginia soil in the first Battle of Bull Run, and Robert E. Lee had been commissioned as a brigadier general in the Confederate Army.

While Lincoln appears to have regarded the secession of Virginia and North Carolina as inevitable, he was determined to keep the border states of Maryland, Kentucky,

Tennessee, and Missouri in the Union, especially Kentucky,[14] where he had been born. In April 1861 Kentucky adopted a policy of neutrality, remaining in the Union but supporting neither Lincoln's war to suppress the rebellion nor the Confederates' military response. Given this extremely delicate situation, Lincoln moved swiftly to shore up support for pro-Union elements in Kentucky. In May he created a new Military Department of Kentucky, which he placed under the command of the newly minted brigadier general Robert Anderson, hero of Fort Sumter and a Kentuckian by birth.[15] Lincoln also approved the distribution of rifles and ammunition to pro-Union militias. Anderson, who was reluctant to support the arming of civilians, urged caution. When Confederate forces crossed into Kentucky, Anderson left his headquarters in Cincinnati to appear before the legislature in Frankfort, which at his urging adopted a formal demand that the Confederates withdraw their troops.[16] Kentucky thus chose to remain in the Union, though many of its citizens fought on the Confederate side. The eminent Civil War historian Shelby Foote gives credit largely to Robert Anderson for this strategically critical outcome.[17] Lincoln nevertheless requested his resignation from command of the Military Department of Kentucky (which included the newly formed Army of Ohio) in the fall of 1861. Lincoln's close friend in Kentucky, Joshua Speed, met with Anderson and then on October 7, 1861, wrote Lincoln that Anderson "seemed grieved that [he] had to surrender his command . . . [but] agreed that it was necessary and gracefully yielded."[18] By then Anderson's health was broken and he spent the remainder of the war in New

York City, where he could be "pointed out on the avenue as he took his daily constitutional, still the hero of Sumter, wearing a long military cloak across his shoulders to hide his stars."[19] Thus ended Robert Anderson's Civil War career, though he retained his standing as one of the Union's first celebrated heroes.

Having escaped from Texas with his wife and children in the fall of 1861, Charles Anderson was not to be overshadowed by his famous older brother. Shortly after his return to Ohio, Anderson called on Abraham Lincoln in Washington and offered his services in aid of the Union cause. Lincoln thereupon dispatched Anderson on a tour of Great Britain to argue the case for the war to restore the Union in a series of public talks. It is a measure of Anderson's stature that the president chose him for arguably the most important and sensitive diplomatic mission of the day, as the Confederate government was engaged in an all-out effort to gain the support of Great Britain for its cause. Paying his own way, Anderson sailed for Britain on March 29, 1862.[20] According to one biographer, Anderson's "mission was short and fruitless," and after delivering a number of insignificant speeches and taking a week-long holiday in France, he returned to the United States.[21]

When Charles Anderson returned to Ohio, the governor was attempting to fill the federally assigned quota of enlistments in the Union army, and to fill the decimated ranks following the bloody Battle of Shiloh. He turned to Anderson, who recruited almost a thousand men to form the new 93rd Ohio Volunteer Infantry, which mustered in Dayton in August 1862 under the command of Anderson, a newly commissioned colonel. When the regiment departed for Lexington, Kentucky, on August 23, 1862, it numbered 39 officers and 929 men under Colonel Anderson's command.[22] In the fall of 1862 the 93rd Ohio was assigned to the 3rd Brigade of the 2nd Division in the corps commanded by General Alexander McCook in the Union Army of the Cumberland.

This western Union army had originally been organized in 1861 under the name "Army of Ohio," and, as noted above, its first commanding general was Charles Anderson's older brother Robert. It is unknown what role or influence Robert may have had or exerted in the appointment of his younger brother to command the 93rd Ohio. When the Union forces in the west were reorganized in 1862, General William Rosecrans assumed command of what had been the Army of Ohio and rechristened it the Army of the Cumberland. In December 1862 Rosecrans was maneuvering his large army, which numbered approximately forty-four thousand men, in Middle Tennessee in the hope of finding and attacking the Confederate Army of Tennessee commanded by General Braxton Bragg, which had been formed in November 1862.[23] The two armies collided at Stones River outside Murfreesboro, Tennessee, early on the morning of December 31, 1862. Rosecrans intended to attack Bragg with his superior Union forces and inflict a major defeat that would boost Northern morale after the devastating defeat suffered three weeks earlier by the Union Army of the Potomac at the Battle of Fredericksburg in Virginia. As it happened, however, the Confederate commander had also decided to launch a flanking attack on Rosecrans's forces. Bragg hurled his infantry brigades against the right wing of Rosecrans's army at the crack of dawn, while the Union troops were cooking a leisurely breakfast before initiating their own attack.[24] The Union right wing, which incorporated Charles Anderson's 93rd Ohio, commanded by General McCook, was overrun by the Confederate infantry and fell back in disarray. Only the spirited defense fought by the Union division commanded by General Philip Sheridan prevented a complete rout. Rosecrans was able to re-form his forces in a strong defensive position, which repulsed repeated Confederate assaults over the next several days. The Battle of Stones River[25] was one of the largest and bloodiest of the Civil War, with a total of 24,645 casualties out of 81,713 men engaged, the highest percentage of loss of any major battle in the war.[26]

The 93rd Ohio suffered heavy casualties in the opening phase of the battle. Among those wounded was its commanding officer, Colonel Charles Anderson. Despite his wounds, Anderson composed an after-action report on January 5, 1863, which detailed the dispositions and movements of his regiment and its participation in the fighting on December 31. After describing the commencement of the early-morning Confederate attack, Anderson wrote:

> I ordered the skirmishers to rally on the right wing, which had not yet begun its deployment, and the colonel commanding the brigade then gave me orders, in person, to retreat. . . . The regiment, like the rest of the retreating troops, of course much increase[d] its speed, so that by the time it passed out of the woods into the cotton-field to the northward the march had degenerated into a run.

> At this point, and in the cotton-field, the men of my regiment suffered quite severely. Notwithstanding, however, the number of killed, wounded, and scattered, a small remnant of the Ninety-third Ohio was rallied with those of the division . . . and formed in line of battle in the large woods. . . . This line . . . marched a short distance against the enemy, which by this time . . . were again flanking our right in very great force.

Anderson concluded his report by noting his "temporary absence from my regiment, in order to have two slight wounds looked at and dressed by a surgeon" and then wrote that "these little and trivial details [are] seen to make a sufficient record of my regiment's share in these great proceedings."[27]

Anderson shed greater light on the seriousness of his wounds and the conduct of the right wing of Rosecrans's army at Stones River in a letter he wrote to his daughter within days following the battle.[28] "Dearest Daughter," he wrote, "I have nothing new to say of myself—except that I have been so unwell, feverish and in pain from my wound, that I was on the verge of asking sick-leave." He continued:

> Yesterday and the day before (the day after Genl McCook left) I was especially sick. The Dr thought I was tending to typhoid fever. But I think the danger has passed and I am of an upward tendency again. . . . My wound, however, kept me awake last night by extreme tenderness and pain without being seriously hurt. . . . It is very small, but like an Irishman's pig very active in the count. I confess great disgust at it.

> I sent to you and Belle my suit of clothes, "marred as you see by the traitors"—with the bullet that hit me on the hip. . . . I confess myself really vexed and sorry at this misadventure—since nothing else but the holes . . . could show the wondrous escape of the wearer.

After commenting on the possibility of a renewed Confederate attack and the apparent controversy over General Rosecrans's "censure" of his subordinates at Stones River, Anderson offered his daughter this interesting explanation for the collapse of the right wing of the Union army:

> I am now inclined to believe, that we were simply overwhelmed by superior numbers, thrown with sudden and excellent strategy upon our weakest point of men . . . after seeing and admitting the admirable plan of their attack . . . if they had not unaccountably failed in vigor in the following it up [they] would have swept us all from the face of the earth, or captured every body and thing not destroyed. . . . I think our Wing—our Division at least—was too far out. The open fields and Air were our only right shield. We were too much "in the Air"—out of doors. The result was, as it was—whether from being surprised or overwhelmed, matters nothing. . . . Taken altogether, we all got out of the snap remarkably well.

Anderson's injury, evidently a bullet wound to the hip, was serious enough that he was unable to return to active duty with his regiment and so resigned his commission and traveled to Ohio in early 1863, by which time both Charles and his brother Robert had risen to national prominence. Having served as Lincoln's special envoy to Great Britain, Charles now returned to his home state as the wounded commander of a regiment of Ohio volunteer infantry that fought in one of the great battles of the war. It is perhaps therefore unsurprising that he chose to return to the realm of Ohio politics, in which he had been active twenty years earlier. And in 1863 politics in Ohio were at a fever pitch, with serious implications for both the outcome of the war and Abraham Lincoln's bid for reelection the following year. As the Confederate Army of Northern Virginia, now under the command of Robert E. Lee, won a series of conspicuous victories over its larger and better-equipped Union adversary in 1862 and the spring of 1863, support was building in the North for a negotiated end to the war and its terrible bloodshed.

The leader of the so-called Peace Democrats, or "copperheads," who favored an end to the war, was a handsome congressman from Dayton, Ohio, named Clement Vallandigham. In the spring of 1863 Vallandigham was seeking election as governor of Ohio as a Democrat, a position from which, if elected, he intended to mount a bid to unseat Abraham Lincoln in 1864. Union general Ambrose Burnside, who had commanded the Army of the Potomac in its disastrous defeat at the Battle of Fredericksburg in December 1862, had been reassigned to command the Department of the Ohio, which consisted of the states bordering the Ohio River. Burnside issued his infamous General Order No. 38 in April 1863, stating that "the habit of declaring sympathies for the enemy" would not be tolerated in the Department of the Ohio and providing that anyone who committed "expressed or implied" treason would be put on trial before a military tribunal and, if found guilty, would be subject to punishment by death or banishment. Vallandigham promptly decided to put to the test an order of such dubious legality. Speaking at a political rally in Ohio on May 1, Vallandigham declared the war to be "wicked, cruel, and unnecessary," and its object "crushing out liberty and erecting a despotism" and creating "a war for the freedom of the blacks and the enslavement of the whites."[29] Burnside took the bait and sent a party of Union troops to break down the door of Vallandigham's home in Dayton in the middle of the night and place him under arrest before his wailing wife.[30] At a trial before a military tribunal on May 6 and 7, Vallandigham was found guilty of violating General Order No. 38 and sentenced to confinement in a military prison for the duration of the war. Burnside's arrest and conviction of Vallandigham provoked widespread outrage across the North. Rather than have him imprisoned, Lincoln sent Vallandigham under military escort across the Confederate lines outside Murfreesboro, Tennessee, whence he made his way to coastal North Carolina and boarded a fast blockade runner to Canada. Thus Vallandigham was able to resume his campaign for Ohio governor from the safety of Ontario.[31]

During the Civil War era governors of Ohio served a two-year term, with elections held in odd-numbered years. Voters also elected a lieutenant governor, and candidates for that office did not run on a ticket with the gubernatorial candidate and could even be from a different political party. The lieutenant governor would succeed a governor who resigned or died in office. In 1863 the Ohio Republicans chose a heavyset politician and newspaperman named John Brough (which rhymed with "rough") to oppose Vallandigham for the state's highest office. And as their candidate for lieutenant governor, the Republicans chose Charles Anderson. In his curious campaign waged from Canada, Vallandigham hammered on the Peace Democrats' opposition to continuance of the war as the folly of radical New England abolitionists, which was bankrupting the country, and to Lincoln's "tyrannical" measures such as conscription and suspension of the writ of habeas

Clement Vallandigham. (Wikipedia, "Clement Vallandigham," http://en.wikipedia.org/wiki/Clement_Vallandigham)

corpus. Unlikely as it seems from today's vantage point, Vallandigham argued that the war should end with the readmission of the Confederate States to the Union, with the institution of slavery preserved, an outcome Confederate leaders were not seeking.[32] With widespread opposition to the draft in the North and the enormous loss of life in the war, there was nevertheless strong popular support for the Democrats, especially in the midwestern states of Ohio, Indiana, and even Lincoln's home state of Illinois.

As the Ohio governor's race entered late summer, Vallandigham's support began to dwindle in the wake of the capture of Vicksburg by the Union forces commanded by U. S. Grant and Lee's failed attempt to inflict a decisive defeat on the Union army at Gettysburg. The tone of Vallandigham's campaign, now that Lincoln had decreed the emancipation of the slaves, was increasingly racist, with Democrats characterizing the election as an "irrepressible conflict between white and black laborers," arguing that "every vote [should] count in favor of the *white* man and against the Abolitionist hordes."[33] Because of his impressive girth, the Republican candidate Brough was ridiculed as a "fat Knight of the corps d'Afrique."[34] Large numbers of Ohio voters were men fighting in the numerous volunteer regiments who were determined to see the war to a successful victory over the Rebels. And almost all of them were able to vote in the governor's race, which had become a virtual referendum on the war and Lincoln's conduct of it. When the day of the election arrived, Brough was elected governor and Charles Anderson as lieutenant governor by large majorities. Brough's victory over Vallandigham prompted

Abraham Lincoln to send a telegram to the governor-elect stating: "Glory to God in the Highest. Ohio has saved the nation."[35]

Shortly after the election, it was announced that a ceremony dedicating a cemetery for the Union dead in the Battle of Gettysburg would be held on November 19, 1863, at the site of the battle. Each state whose troops had fought there for the Union was requested to send a delegation, and among those traveling to the ceremony on behalf of Ohio were governor-elect John Brough and lieutenant governor-elect Charles Anderson. Moreover, Anderson, who by then had acquired a reputation as an orator, was requested to deliver a public address. The keynote address before the large gathering assembled at Gettysburg was delivered by Edward Everett, a Unitarian minister and former president of Harvard College who was widely regarded as a great orator. In the style of public speakers of the day, Everett delivered a two-hour-long address replete with allusions to the classics and high-flown patriotic sentiment. At the conclusion of Everett's oration, Lincoln rose and delivered his brief, remarkable address, described merely as "dedicatory remarks" in the ceremony's program. After the ceremony, the Ohio delegation repaired to the Gettysburg Presbyterian Church on Baltimore Street, where by prearrangement Charles Anderson was to address the gathering.[36] Among those in attendance were President Lincoln and Secretary of State Seward.

Treated to "rousing cheers," Anderson rose to speak. While Lincoln's Gettysburg address, a few words of dedication that he hastily composed and revised on the train trip from Washington, has gone down as arguably the most famous speech in history, Anderson's address utterly disappeared from history as soon as he delivered it. The text was discovered by happenstance in 2002 at the Wyoming ranch house of Bartley Skinner, a great-grandson of Charles Anderson who had several cardboard boxes filled with Anderson's personal papers. Among the documents was an undated and untitled "thirty-nine page manuscript written in dark brown ink on a gray-lined legal pad."[37] Described as "fiery and provocative," in contrast to Lincoln's solemn and inspirational prose, Anderson's address was a call to arms exhorting the Union to finish the job of crushing the hated Southern rebellion.[38] He denounced the Confederates as "that host of rebels, deluded and sent hither by conspirators and traitors [who] were vanquished and fled cowering in dismay from this land of Penn and Franklin—of Peace and Freedom—across the Potomac into the domain of Calhoun and Davis—of oligarchic rule and despotic oppression."[39] Anderson castigated the leaders of the South as men "who were born into the inheritance of unjust power; nurtured by the milk of slaves and slavery, rocked in their cradle by servile hands . . . cultured into morbid activities and pampered, at last, into insane, parricidal, suicidal arrogance." Referring to the fallen Union soldiers, Anderson exclaimed that "their blood cries out from all this beloved ground, to all these wide heavens above, for God has heard that cry" and warned that "a yet bloodier retribution awaits—nay now falls upon—those wretched men, whose crime neither Earth can hide nor the seas can cleanse." In what must have been a deeply disturbing declaration to Lincoln, Anderson vowed, "Let them seize and destroy our National City—its wood into ashes and its marble into sand. Let them imprison—hang—burn our President with all the heads and hands of the departments. . . . Yet we are still a nation!" According to Anderson biographer David Dixon, Anderson's oration was greeted with wild cheering, and after speaking for just under an hour, he was warmly congratulated by President Lincoln.[40] Following their return to Ohio, John Brough was sworn into office as governor and Charles Anderson as lieutenant governor in January 1864.

The Civil War ended on April 9, 1865, with the surrender of Robert E. Lee's Army of Northern Virginia to General U. S. Grant at Appomattox Court House. Five days later, on April 14, four years to the day after his surrender of the Union garrison at Fort Sumter, Brigadier General Robert Anderson returned to Charleston to preside at the ceremonial raising of the Stars and Stripes over Fort Sumter.[41] Among the large crowd attending the ceremony was one Robert Vesey, an emancipated African American slave, whose father, Denmark Vesey, had famously been executed in Charleston in 1822 for having led a failed slave insurrection.[42] The presence of the younger Vesey at the Fort Sumter flag-raising no doubt sent a powerful message to the white citizens of Charleston, and the South, about the restoration of federal control over the defeated states of the Confederacy. And on the night of April 14, 1865, President Abraham Lincoln was mortally wounded at Ford's Theatre by John Wilkes Booth.

John Brough was destined not to complete his two-year term as governor of Ohio. Several months after the end of the Civil War, Brough fell and injured his leg, which became infected and resulted in his death on August 29, 1865. On that date Charles Anderson, having fled Texas and left behind his large home overlooking the Olmos Basin in San Antonio four years earlier, became the twenty-seventh governor of Ohio. After serving the remainder of Brough's term, Anderson did not seek reelection but retired to private life in January 1866. He returned to Dayton to practice law until moving in 1870 to his native state of Kentucky, where he died at the age of eighty-one on September 2, 1895. After returning to Ohio in the fall of 1861 he never again laid eyes on his beloved Texas home, which in time would be known as the Argyle.

Charles Anderson as governor of Ohio. (Capitol Square Review and Advisory Board, Ohio Statehouse; image courtesy of Garth's Auctioneers and Appraisers, Delaware, Ohio)

3

The McLane Years

All through the tumultuous years of the Civil War, Charles Anderson's hilltop house in San Antonio sat empty. Although Anderson had sold the house and surrounding property to William McLane in September 1861, McLane apparently did not occupy the property until after the war. At some time the house was reputedly occupied by Confederate troops who used it as an arsenal to store weapons and ammunition.[1] For this reason, and also because Anderson had built the house on what was referred to as the "Arsenal Lot," for years after the war, the hill on which it stands was known as "Arsenal Hill." William McLane, like Anderson a native of Kentucky, first came to Texas in 1812 to take part in the ill-fated Gutiérrez-Magee Expedition,[2] a so-called filibuster in which American volunteers joined forces with Mexican revolutionaries seeking to overthrow Spanish colonial rule in Texas as a part of the broader Mexican War of Independence. Consigned to the dustbins of history,[3] the Gutiérrez-Magee Expedition was an important episode in nineteenth-century Texas history and in the Mexican war with Spain and, arguably, was a precursor to the events of 1836 that led to Texas independence. A combined American-Mexican force, jointly commanded by José Bernardo Gutiérrez de Lara and Augustus W. Magee, departed from Nacogdoches in 1812 for South Texas and scored military victories over royalist forces at Goliad and San Antonio, in the Battle of Rosillo, or Salado Creek, before being routed in 1813 in the Battle of Medina.[4] One of a small number of American survivors of the filibuster, McLane departed Texas for Indiana, where his son Hiram H. McLane was born in 1820.

William McLane and his son Hiram moved to Texas in 1858 and bought a ranch near Helena, now a ghost town but then the county seat of Karnes County. Three years later the

William McLane. (TBRI)

elder McLane purchased Charles Anderson's large house and 128 acres. According to one report, shortly after the end of the Civil War Hiram McLane married Emma Hurd of New York.[5] While it is unclear when the McLane family first occupied the old Anderson home, in the spring of 1866 William McLane was attempting to sell it, placing an advertisement in the *San Antonio Express* offering

> that very desirable residence situated at the head of the river known as the Anderson Place. It is certainly one of the prettiest and loveliest country seats in western Texas, situated four miles north of San Antonio, comprising one-hundred and twenty-eight acres of land with stone house sixty feet square, with eleven rooms, good cistern, stone corrals, 40 acres under fence, ten of which are rich bottom in cultivation.[6]

With the Texas economy devastated in the aftermath of the war, there were no takers for McLane's offer to sell. For the next twenty-three years, the old "Anderson Place" was home to Hiram and Emma McLane and their son Hiram Howard, daughter Zula Elma, and ward Maud Coffman, who was Emma's niece. Hiram's father, William, also lived there until his death in 1873. In addition to the house and ranch, McLane evidently also acquired Anderson's sorrel horses, including the stallions named for figures from the Old Testament. Shortly after the war McLane began breeding horses for the US Army, which had resumed cavalry operations on the Texas frontier against the Comanche and Kiowa. McLane's horses, known as the Circle Dot, were considered "the finest cavalry horses," as McLane "crossed the light fast horses he brought to the ranch with the tough sorrels that Anderson left behind to produce a rugged breed that great Indian fighters like General John Lapham Bullis used in preference to any others."[7] Neither William nor Hiram McLane resembled the typical rough-and-tumble nineteenth-century Texas rancher and frontiersman. Both men were educated and literate, with a penchant for writing and a passionate interest in Texas's struggle for independence from Mexico. William McLane authored a serious account of the filibuster against the Spanish colonial forces, which was reprinted in 1963 by the *Southwestern Historical Quarterly* under the title "William McLane's Narrative of the Magee-Gutierrez Expedition, 1812–1813."[8] Hiram McLane was a collector of rare books and violins and indulged a strong interest in writing fiction, poetry, and drama. According to one account, McLane's violin collection numbered twenty-six, one of which was reputed to be a Stradivarius.[9] His father's narrative of the Gutiérrez-Magee Expedition provided the basis for Hiram's novel *Irene Viesca,* which was published by the San Antonio Printing Company in 1886. Hiram dedicated the lengthy volume (547 pages) "to my departed Father, some of the romantic incidents in the history of whose life have furnished the basis for my story." The novel is a detailed description of the Gutiérrez-Magee Expedition based entirely on William McLane's account. The author noted that "the narrative as given herein is just as it came from his pen." In the same year (1886), Hiram McLane's fanciful drama *The Capture of the Alamo* was released by the same publisher. Though the slender book can be read as an account of the siege of the Alamo written in blank verse, McLane intended it as a stage production, stating in the preface that it was "written to be placed upon the *boards*." When that evidently failed to materialize, he decided to offer it as a book "to be sold for the purpose of raising funds to erect a suitable monument on the spot where they fell to the band of noble men who sacrificed their lives for their country."[10] It is unknown whether McLane actually raised any funds for such a monument from the sale of the book (the actual monument, the Alamo Cenotaph, was not erected for another fifty years, in 1936).

In McLane's fanciful retelling of the Alamo saga, the figure of Davy Crockett was presented as a legendary folk hero speaking in a backwoods dialect so bizarre it would

Hiram McLane with his wife, Emma, and ward Maud Coffman. (TBRI)

have made the writers of the 1950s television drama cringe. Here is Crockett fending off the Mexican troops who have overrun the mission:

> Bring on yer lioners and tigers
> yer cattermounts and allergaters
> fer I'm er half hoss and half allergater myself, I ar;
> Bring on yer sea hoss, yer red hoss, and yer land terrapin,
> yer white bar, yer black bar, and yer grizler bar,
> yer big fish, yer leetle fish, and yer whales,
> yer boer-constrictors, yer snappin' turtles and tad poles,
> yer black-and-tans, yer gray hounds, and yer terriers,
> yer bob-tail cats, yer long-tail cats, and yer ring-tail roarers.
> Who tis yer wants ter lick, does yer?
> Wall, then I'll tell yer.
> It ar old Davy Crockett, o' Tennessee, it ar.
> And yer wants to tuk up
> this har fite yerself, does yer?[11]

Alas, in the play's closing scene Davy confronts Santa Anna himself and, failing to recognize him, is slain by a volley of Mexican musket fire. At the end of the book is an engraving with the caption "Col. William McLane, who died at his residence, at the head of the San Antonio river, adjoining the city limits of San Antonio, Texas, May 11, 1873, and who was the last of the Magee expedition, which expedition aided materially in securing the freedom of Mexico from Spanish rule, and which ultimately led to the independence of Texas." It is easy to imagine the erudite Hiram McLane at

The old Anderson Place in the 1880s. (TBRI)

The McLane home and grandchildren in the late 1880s. (TBRI)

his writing desk in the large sixty-by-sixty antebellum home built by Charles Anderson, penning his fanciful poetry. McLane was also an amateur Texas historian who made the direct connection between the Magee filibuster's attempt to wrest Texas from Spanish rule and the noble struggle at the Alamo and ultimate Texas independence from Mexico twenty-three years later.

According to some reports, during the 1870s the McLanes rented out rooms in their large house to boarders, some of whom were Northerners spending the mild winters in San Antonio. By 1888, Hiram McLane, approaching the age of seventy and with grown children, decided to sell his hilltop home and property. By then the cavalry's long-running war with the Indians had ended and the city of San Antonio was growing rapidly, expanding northward into the scenic hills at the mouth of the river. At some point after the death of his father in 1873, Hiram had acquired a substantial amount of land adjoining the original 128 Anderson acres. In 1875 he purchased land in the vicinity from George W. Brackenridge, the most notable figure in the city during the decades following the Civil War.

Brackenridge, a native of Indiana, attended Hanover College before moving to Texas in the 1850s to go into business with his father and brother.[12] Having tired of business, Brackenridge enrolled in Harvard Law School in the fall of 1860. When Texas voted to secede, Brackenridge withdrew from Harvard to return to Texas.[13] Like Charles Anderson, Brackenridge opposed secession and the Confederacy, but unlike Anderson, he remained in Texas during the conflict and made a large fortune in the trade Mexicans referred to as "Los Algodones"—selling contraband cotton from the Gulf Coast port of Matamoros for shipment to New York.[14] Though he was eventually expelled from Texas by Confederate forces, later in the war he held an important position for the US Treasury Department in New Orleans, which was under federal control.[15] By the end of the war Brackenridge had amassed a fortune estimated at $100,000 from the shipment of Texas cotton to agents in New York.[16] Following the war, Brackenridge lived the rest of his long life in San Antonio as a wealthy bachelor, expanding his fortune in banking, real estate, and the newspaper business.[17] He purchased several hundred acres adjoining McLane's property, which included the "Old Sweet Place," a home built by James R. Sweet, mayor of San Antonio in the 1850s. Brackenridge enlarged the house into a beautiful three-story Victorian, which he named "Fernridge." Also located on Brackenridge's property was the remarkable artesian well known as the Blue Hole, described by the famous landscape architect Frederick Law Olmsted in 1856 as

> the first water among the gems of the natural world. The whole river gushes up in one sparkling burst from the earth. It has all the beautiful accompaniments of a smaller spring, moss, pebbles, seclusion, sparkling sunbeams, and dense overhanging luxuriant foliage. The effect is overpowering.[18]

The Blue Hole, where limestone-filtered water from the Edwards Aquifer surfaces to form the San Antonio River, produced a prodigious flow of cool, limpid water that

Brackenridge harnessed to supply the drinking water for the city in the 1880s through his privately owned San Antonio Water Works Company. And it was Brackenridge who coined the name "Alamo Heights" for the neighborhood encompassing his property and the adjoining McLane lands, with their rolling hills, limestone cliffs, and ancient live oaks. Brackenridge eventually sold over two hundred acres to the Sisters of Charity of the Incarnate Word, who renamed Fernridge the Brackenridge Villa and established a convent and later a Catholic college. Brackenridge donated the balance of his Alamo Heights acreage to the city of San Antonio in 1899 to establish Brackenridge Park, the city's principal public park.[19]

By the late 1880s it must have been clear to Hiram McLane that the future of his landholdings no longer lay in horse breeding for the army but in residential development. Thus on May 2, 1889, McLane sold "about 1,500 acres lying north of the city at the head of the San Antonio River" for the impressive sum of $150,000 to Charles W. Ogden, W. J. Ballantyne Patterson, and R.W. Russell.[20] The sale included the McLane home place on Arsenal Hill. The three named purchasers were representatives of the Chamberlain Investment Company, a Denver-based land developer. On August 11, 1890, Ogden, Patterson, and Russell sold the 1,500 acres to the Alamo Heights Land and Improvement Company, a newly formed Colorado corporation of which Patterson was president and general manager, for $1 million, resulting in a profit of $850,000 to the sellers in a period of fifteen months. The Alamo Heights Land and Improve-

George Brackenridge's home "Fernridge." (Photo by author)

ment Company engaged an engineer named Bob Salter[21] to lay out and plat a large subdivision of residential lots called "Alamo Heights," with streets following the natural contours of the hilly topography, which was recorded on January 29, 1891. The original subdivision extended from Arsenal Hill, overlooking the Olmos Basin on the west, and bordered the Brackenridge property to the south (later sold to the Sisters of Charity), east to what today is Broadway, and north to Ogden Avenue. One of the principal streets, forming a loop along the boundary with the Brackenridge property and following the contour of the hills to the west and then back to the east, was named Patterson Avenue. Included in the original plat was block number 26, consisting of 1.2587 acres, the Arsenal Lot on which Charles Anderson had built his home in 1860, now situated on Patterson Avenue.

4
The Argyle Hotel

> High on its hill, the Argyle still stands,
> a monument not only to the past, but to
> good living and good taste.
>
> —Alice O'Grady, *The Argyle Cookbook*

Having platted Alamo Heights, W. J. Ballantyne Patterson decided to convert the McLane-Anderson home on block 26 into an inn and dining establishment, which he christened the "Argyle Hotel," reputedly because the hilltop setting reminded him of the Argyllshire countryside of his Scottish forebears. But first Patterson significantly enlarged and modified the structure built by Anderson, adding a third story and a wide portico at the front with distinctive pillars, but retaining the original sixty-by-sixty-foot building with its thick limestone walls and elevated entrance. According to an account in the *San Antonio Light* in 1940, Patterson "placed in charge of the hotel . . . a family named Carr, of which Mrs. Lucy Tobin Carr . . . was co-manager." Mrs. Carr was the sister of John W. Tobin, who later served as sheriff of Bexar County and as mayor of San Antonio in the 1920s. The article in the *Light* continued: "After a year of no success the Carrs left the hotel vacant."[1] With the departure of the Carrs, Patterson turned to a brother and sister named Robert and Alice O'Grady, who had managed a roadside inn at the small town of Boerne, northwest of San Antonio. They were the son and daughter of one John G. O'Grady, who was born in 1829 in Westport, Ireland, and emigrated to Boston in 1848. He served a stint as a sergeant in the US Army at Fort McKavett in Menard, Texas, one of the outposts established in the 1850s to battle the Indians, where he met and married Katherine Cahill, an Irishwoman from Tipperary. After O'Grady left the army, he and his wife arrived in Boerne in 1859.[2]

Boerne in 1859 was a tiny settlement thirty miles northwest of San Antonio that had been settled largely by German immigrants. The area was valued for its scenic hills, pleasant climate, and abundant clean water from Cibolo Creek. A leading German American doctor in San Antonio named Ferdinand Herff advised patients suffering from tuberculosis to move to Boerne for "its clean mountain air," and the town was becoming popular for those seeking a cure or escaping San Antonio's oppressive summer heat.[3] Described as "a red-headed, loud and jolly fellow," John O'Grady built an adobe inn and boardinghouse called the Kendall House Inn on the banks of the creek where the Camino Viejo, the highway from San Antonio, entered the town.[4] According to his daughter Alice, John O'Grady "opened a stage station, where travelers might dine while the horses were being changed."[5] The inn also provided overnight accommodations to travelers "and the handful of consumptives who were starting to trickle into town on Dr. Herff's orders."[6] One of O'Grady's overnight guests was Robert E. Lee, who was returning to San Antonio before the outbreak of the Civil War.[7] Bob and Alice O'Grady acquired their experience and skills as innkeepers in their youth and early adulthood at their father's Kendall House Inn.

By the 1890s Boerne had waned in popularity as a resort destination for visitors from San Antonio, which might explain why the O'Grady siblings decided to take on the management of the new Argyle Hotel following the failed efforts of the Carrs. In almost all published accounts of the Argyle's history, Bob and Alice O'Grady are reported to have purchased the hotel in 1893 from two unnamed Scotsmen who had bought the property and converted it into a hotel. This is attributable to Alice O'Grady's own account in *The Argyle Cookbook*, which was published in 1940. In it, Alice, with her coauthor Monte Barrett, wrote:

> In 1890 the [McLane] ranch was purchased by the Chamberlain Investment Company of Denver, which employed Bob Salter, an engineer, to lay out Alamo Heights for speculative purposes. The ranch house was sold to two Scots, who added the third floor, employed a man named Carr to operate it, and opened the hotel, which they named Argyle because the rolling hills . . . reminded them of their native hills in Scotland. Their venture did not flourish, and they shortly sold out to the O'Grady's, who opened the hotel, under their management, on St. Patrick's Day 1893.[8]

In fact, when the O'Gradys came on board to manage the Argyle, the hotel was owned by the Alamo Heights Land and Improvement Company, whose president was W. J. B. Patterson. As noted above, the Scotsman who modified the building and conceived the name "Argyle" was in fact Patterson, who evidently was of Scottish birth or descent. Bob and Alice O'Grady did reopen the hotel for business on Saint Patrick's Day (appropriately, given the land of their parents' birth) in 1893 but did not purchase the property until 1906, thirteen years later. The discrepancies may have been due to Alice O'Grady's dimmed memory in 1940 (she was an octogenarian), or she may have been ignorant of the facts.

In any case, beginning in March 1893 the O'Grady siblings operated the Argyle for the next five decades as a hotel and dining establishment known for its sumptuous Southern cuisine and elegant appointments. It is this period—the O'Grady years—that established the Argyle's enduring image and reputation as a great antebellum mansion embodying all the qualities and charms (or myths) of the Old South. From her brief history included at the beginning of *The Argyle Cookbook*, it is apparent that "Miss Alice"—she never married—carefully cultivated this image. She wrote that the cookbook contained "the rich recipes of the storied South . . . part of the prodigal days of plenty before the War Between the States," which she referred to as "the Lost Cause."[9] It is no small irony that the only antebellum phase of the Argyle's history was the brief interval when Charles Anderson, a determined pro-Union Yankee, future Union army colonel and governor of Ohio, and brother of the hero of Fort Sumter, resided there with his wife and children.

Little is known of the early years of the Argyle Hotel under the management of "Miss Alice" and "Mr. Bob," as the O'Gradys were evidently addressed. The Alamo Heights subdivision was ahead of its time and languished. Few lots were sold and fewer houses built in the last decade of the nineteenth century and first decade of the twentieth. The great majority of San Antonio's inhabitants lived in neighborhoods far to the south, near what is today downtown, with the old Spanish colonial landmarks of the Alamo, San Fernando Cathedral, Military Plaza, and the governor's residence. Most of the affluent citizens lived south of Commerce Street near the San Antonio River in neighborhoods like the King William district[10] with its impressive limestone Victorian mansions.

The new Argyle Hotel was, however, relatively close to Fort Sam Houston, the sprawling army post whose original structure—the Quadrangle—was completed in 1879. From its beginnings in 1859, the Argyle's history had been closely tied to the presence of the US Army in San Antonio. At the end of the Civil War, some 4,600 Union troops were stationed in San Antonio under the command of the Army's Fifth District.[11] Though the Civil War resulted in an interlude in the cavalry's long-running war with the Comanche, the fighting resumed with a vengeance at the war's end. By the early 1870s city leaders were pressing the War Department in Washington to establish a permanent army post in San Antonio. In 1876 President Grant approved the construction of the post, the army acquired a site of several hundred acres northeast of the city, and construction began on the Quadrangle, a large rectangular limestone structure with an eighty-seven-foot-tall clock tower at the center of the interior courtyard.[12] The post expanded rapidly, with some sixty buildings added between 1885 and 1891 on the periphery of a large parade ground. In 1890 the secretary of war directed that the post be designated "Fort Sam Houston." During the first decade of the twentieth century, Georgian Revival–style housing was constructed for officers' housing as well as a one-thousand-bed hospital.[13] Many buildings completed in 1908 were built in the distinctive "Canal Zone" style, three stories with exterior limestone walls, wood and masonry columns, and enclosed

"Miss Alice" O'Grady. (From *The Argyle Cookbook*)

verandas on the first and second stories, in reference to the army's major construction projects in Panama during the same period.[14]

With the opening of the Argyle Hotel in 1893 relatively close to what soon came to be called "Fort Sam," Miss Alice's Southern cooking and the hotel's gracious public rooms, veranda, and grounds soon became popular with senior army officers and their wives. Though many notable officers are known to have frequented the Argyle during the late nineteenth and early twentieth centuries, there is no record of Teddy Roosevelt having done so during the weeks he spent in San Antonio in May 1898 training and equipping the Rough Riders to fight in Cuba in the Spanish-American War. This motley collection of cowhands and Indian fighters from Texas and the Arizona and Oklahoma Territories and wealthy sportsmen from the Northeast was assembled under the command of Colonel Leonard Wood, an army surgeon who had recently befriended Roosevelt, the young assistant secretary of the navy.[15] With the formation of the Rough Riders (officially the 1st US Volunteer Cavalry), Roosevelt resigned from the Navy Department, was commissioned a lieutenant colonel, and joined Wood in San Antonio. The amateur soldiers were encamped at the fairgrounds at Riverside Park, near the Spanish missions south of downtown, and trained on horses supplied by the army quartermaster at Fort Sam before entraining for Tampa, Florida, and shipping out to Cuba.[16] Although there is no indication that TR visited the Argyle, he is reputed to have spent several nights at the Menger Hotel.

Generals John Pershing and Fred Grant. (Wikipedia, "John J. Pershing," https://en.wikipedia.org/wiki/John_J._Pershing; "Frederick Dent Grant," https://en.wikipedia.org/wiki/Frederick_Dent_Grant)

According to Alice O'Grady, the Argyle was a popular dining spot during these years for many senior army officers, as it had been to an earlier generation of officers during the brief period of Anderson's ownership before the Civil War. Miss Alice later wrote: "Most of the army's great have been familiar with Argyle cuisine, from General Bullis [and] 'Fighting Bob' Shafter. . . . General Pershing frequently dined at the Argyle . . . as did General Fred Funston."[17] General John Lapham Bullis had the moniker "Thunderbolt of the Texas Frontier," and the controversial General Funston had led the army's brutal war with the Filipino rebels following the Spanish-American War.[18] General John "Black Jack" Pershing commanded the army's Punitive Expedition into northern Mexico to battle Pancho Villa in 1916. He was then given command of the army's Southern Department, headquartered at Fort Sam, following the death of Funston, where in April 1917 Woodrow Wilson named him to command the American Expeditionary Force in France.[19] Another frequent dinner guest at the Argyle during this period was General Fred Grant, the son of Ulysses S. Grant.[20] It is easy to imagine General Grant in one of the Argyle's elegant dining rooms where a portrait of General Robert E. Lee in his Confederate dress uniform is proudly displayed.

Alamo Heights was not only several miles from the center of San Antonio but was difficult to reach. With no public transportation, the only means of traveling there was on horseback or by horse-drawn buggy on winding, dusty or muddy roads. Though Patterson's land development project was a financial failure, the adjoining two hundred–plus acres sold by George Brackenridge in the 1890s to the Sisters of Charity thrived as a convent, where the motherhouse for the nuns was completed in 1900, and the impressive brick and stone Chapel of the Incarnate Word was added in 1907.

By 1906, the Alamo Heights Land and Improvement Company had failed and was reorganized as a new entity named the Alamo Heights Investment Company, whose principals were Judge M. H. Townsend and W. B. Willim.[21] Marcus Hervey Townsend was a prominent lawyer, politician, and financier (the title "Judge" may have been an honorific) who is best known for having authored the legislation authorizing the state's purchase of the Alamo shrine in 1883.[22] Townsend and Willim retained the so-called Loop properties along Patterson Avenue and north to what is today Cambridge Elementary School but sold the remaining acreage to other investors and land developers.[23] On December 18, 1906, Robert O'Grady finally purchased the Argyle Hotel, paying $3,500 to the Alamo Heights Investment Company for the property described as

> that certain tract or parcel of land . . . near the City of San Antonio at the head of the San Antonio River and being part of the original City lot #38 formerly known as the Arsenal Lot which was conveyed by the City of San Antonio to Charles Anderson by deed dated September 20, 1861 [sic] . . . which is designated as block number Twenty Six (#26) upon the subdivision and plat of the property made by the Alamo Heights Land and Improvement Co . . . the said block includes the house and out houses known as the Argyle Hotel.[24]

By 1909, the Alamo Heights Investment Company had sold the Loop properties and most of the land west of Broadway to an individual named Clifton George who had recently arrived in the city from Oklahoma.[25] A year earlier George had acquired the first Ford automobile dealership in San Antonio, which was on property adjacent to the Alamo.[26] According to one account, Clifton George was "a reckless, gutsy hype artist and risk taker" who "bought up . . . most of the acreage west of River Avenue (later Broadway)" and "became the area's main developer."[27] An interesting example of George's promotional flair was an invitation to tea in the Georges' Alamo Heights home, which he and his wife extended to President William Howard Taft and his guest President Porfirio Díaz of Mexico when it was announced that the two heads of state would be meeting in San Antonio in 1909. The invitation was the front-page headline in the August 1, 1909, edition of the *San Antonio Light and Gazette,* which featured an engraving of the two leaders, a copy of the invitation, and a photograph of the impressive George home. "Mr. and Mrs. George," the newspaper reported, "hope that the magnificent view of the city afforded from Alamo Heights . . . will tempt the two presidents and the members of their party for a short call while seeing the city." The temptation was evidently insufficient, as the invitation was not accepted, but the article on the front page of the *Light* extolled the "splendid view" from "the crest of Alamo Heights" and "of the Post [Fort Sam Houston], the city and the country for many miles from the point near the Argyle hotel on the edge of the park."

The O'Gradys' Argyle Hotel was clearly a leading attraction of Alamo Heights during the first two decades of the century. During this period Alamo Heights acquired a reputation as a desirable suburban neighborhood removed from the city's traffic and noise with its lovely hills, vistas, and ancient live oaks. A visitors' guide published in 1913 reported that "probably the most beautiful of all the suburban additions to San Antonio is Alamo Heights. . . . It is traversed by the Alamo Heights–West End Car Line and is reached by way of River Avenue and by passing Brackenridge Park. One of the drives leads to the Country Club and its golf grounds. . . . There are many handsome residences in this suburb."[28] Another publication from this same period included several poems singing the praises of the subdivision, including the following:

> Yes, away from the city with maddening strife
> Secure in a home with baby and wife,
> With no noise or confusion to haunt the long nights,
> Soul and body find repose on fair Alamo Heights.[29]

With such tributes it is little wonder that Alamo Heights prospered during World War I, with the construction of many homes, both impressive mansions on large lots with stately oaks, and numerous small bungalows. Development was no doubt enhanced by the extension of public transportation to the area, beginning with a mule-drawn streetcar line whose route went south along River Avenue and then west on Patterson into the Loop. The developers of the neighborhood had taken care to spare the large

SAN ANTONIO LIGHT AND GAZETTE

TO ENTERTAIN PRESIDENT TAFT HERE

LAMO HEIGHTS HOSTESS INVITES EXECUTIVE AND PRESIDENT DIAZ TO HOME

HERE IS VERY FIRST WELCOME EXTENDED TO HEADS OF TWO GOVERNMENTS

REAL HOME HOSPITALITY PROFFERED STATESMEN IN DELIGHTFUL SUBUR

WILLIAM H. TAFT AND PORFIRIO DIAZ GUESTS OF HONOR

MR. AND MRS. CLIFTON GEORGE

THE PRESIDENT

Society

Prices of Good Things to Eat

THE WOMAN BEAUTIFUL

BEAUTIFUL WOMEN

Miss Frieda Englehardt

AMERICAN ART OF COIFFURE ASSOCIATION

Nadine Face Powder

San Antonio Light and Gazette, August 1, 1909.

live oaks and other trees that gave the area its distinctive charm, including a very large "twin" live oak (with a double trunk) that was left in the center of Patterson Avenue at Torcido. The streetcar line bypassed this massive tree, which acquired the name "Suicide Oak" as the result of the supposed tragic death of a young woman grieving the loss of her lover. According to the September 3, 1911, edition of the *San Antonio Light,* the massive oak, "topping the hill on the west side of the street car loop in Alamo Heights . . . gnarled and hung with moss . . . supported the trolley wire for a distance of 50 feet." The newspaper explained that "a young girl of the city committed suicide beneath it some years ago." When the Suicide Oak was toppled in a storm in 1941, the newspaper described it as "the most famous tree in Bexar County . . . around 300 years old." Its name was ascribed to "a blighted love affair of a motorman" on the streetcar line who had quarreled with his lover and "found her body dangling in a noose from the tree on his first trip the following morning." Disturbingly, the article added that "sundry other blighted lovers took their lives by a variety of means under the same branch."[30]

By the 1920s, access to Alamo Heights had been further enhanced by the creation of the paved Broadway thoroughfare on the site of the old River Avenue and modernization of the streetcar line along the thoroughfare. Alamo Heights was flourishing, with homes standing on most of the original lots, and business was good for Mr. Bob and Miss Alice's Argyle Hotel. In 1922 the original Alamo Heights High School was constructed on Cambridge Oval (today's Cambridge Elementary School). Also in 1922, it was reported that the city of San Antonio intended to annex Alamo Heights to tax its residents to help pay for a $1.6 million dam across the Olmos Basin following the disastrous downtown flooding of the previous year. At a meeting held at the Argyle in June 1922, citizens voted overwhelmingly to reject annexation and to form an incorporated city. The first mayor of the new city of Alamo Heights was the Argyle's proprietor "Mr. Bob" O'Grady. The first meeting of the city council was called to order by Mayor O'Grady on September 7, 1922, at 8:00 p.m. at the Argyle Hotel, where all future council meetings would be held until 1927, when voters approved a bond issue to build a new city hall on Broadway. As reported in the September 8, 1922, edition of the *Alamo Heights Herald*, the first ordinances passed by the council banned the discharge of firearms, the dumping of trash on vacant lots, and the killing of songbirds. The same article reported that "several of the Aldermen and also the press representatives were disappointed that the Council meeting did not include an Argyle dinner."

Indeed, the Argyle's reputation for serving excellent food in an ambience of old Southern graciousness appears to have been its most noteworthy quality during the height of the O'Grady era. In the introduction to her cookbook, Miss Alice explained that she "had been fond of cooking all her life" and "obtained recipes from every housewife who was noted for the excellence of any certain dish." Some previous accounts of the Argyle credit its gastronomic excellence to the "culinary genius" of Miss Alice, who "was noted for her sauces" and "dazzled diners" with each meal.[31] But apparently the real secret to the quality of the meals served at the Argyle was an African American cook named George Bannister, generally known as "Old George," who was employed in the kitchen for thirty-five years beginning in 1893.[32] Bannister's cooking was evidently so highly prized by senior officers at Fort Sam Houston that they arranged for him to avoid being drafted during World War I.[33] Miss

Alice emphasized that the Argyle's cuisine was representative of the Old South, and certain of the recipes included in her cookbook were certainly Southern in origin, including the Louisiana Plantation Dressing, Southern Style Fried Chicken, George's Oyster Soup, and Sweet Potato Croquettes. Most of the cookbook's recipes, however, are for the relatively bland dishes served in most American homes and restaurants during the decades before World War II and are not especially typical of the South. The Argyle was also known for Miss Alice's elaborately decorated wedding cakes, an example of which is included in one of the photographs in her cookbook. An article that appeared in the September 1941 issue of *Southern Home and Garden* observed that "these cakes journeyed to distant cities, traveling in the center of a sheet-draped Pullman berth."[34] Another food

One of Miss Alice's wedding cakes. (From *The Argyle Cookbook*)

writer commented on the fanciful nature of Miss Alice's presentations, noting that she "dyed her mashed potatoes pink, set her congealed salads on beds of pastel-tinted cabbage, [and] garnished her desserts with morning glories."[35]

Miss Alice's cookbook also provides invaluable insight into the decor of the Argyle Hotel during the long period it was under the O'Gradys' management. Photographs reveal dining rooms, bedrooms, and public areas furnished with antique furniture and artwork probably dating from the late nineteenth century. One contemporary account described the Argyle's "antique silver, cutlery, and furniture," which included

> furniture from one of the Dukes of Savoy's palaces in Italy, a French table of the sixteenth century, a German table of the same era, an old bell like you see in pictures, cypress floors one and one-fourth inches thick, canopied beds with antique washstands, a kitchen redolent of Southern hominy and fried chicken, and an aura of antiquity.[36]

Its cuisine, furnishings, and architecture lent the Argyle its distinctive Southern qualities notwithstanding its distinctive Northern origins. For that reason it was chosen as the location and setting for the film *The Warrens of Virginia,* a 1924 Hollywood silent picture about life on a Virginia plantation during the Civil War.[37] Sadly, the leading lady, actress Martha Mansfield, only twenty-four years old, died from burns in a San Antonio hospital during the film's production when her Civil War–era costume of hoopskirts and

Stills from the silent film. *The Warrens of Virginia*. (Fox Film Corporation)

ruffles was accidentally ignited by a lighted match after she climbed into a car outside the Argyle.[38]

We are also afforded a glimpse of the Argyle's appearance during the final years of the O'Grady period thanks to the O'Gradys' efforts to obtain its inclusion in the National Register of Historic Places. This necessitated submitting an application with a number of black-and-white photographs of the Argyle as it appeared in 1936. During the period of the O'Gradys' ownership, the ground floor space beneath the veranda was open (a seated figure can be dimly made out in the photo showing the north elevation). When the renovations to the Argyle were made in 1955–56, this area was enclosed and became the "porch," one of the most popular à la carte dining areas of the Argyle Club. While the 1936

East elevation of the Argyle in 1936. (TBRI)

North elevation of the Argyle in 1936. (TBRI)

Frame addition to the Argyle in 1936. (TBRI)

photographs submitted to the National Register of Historic Places clearly show that the main building had not been modified from W. J. B. Patterson's 1892 expansion, they also reveal a large frame addition at the rear of the building that was constructed at some point during the O'Gradys' ownership, either to add more hotel rooms or as the result of the gradual transformation of the Argyle into a rooming house during the years of its decline during the Great Depression. This large frame addition was removed during the renovations of 1955–56, which returned the Argyle to its original 1890s design.

By 1940, both the Argyle and its sibling owners had reached ripe old age, and the glory days were at an end. Like so many American institutions and households, the Argyle suffered badly during the Depression. In June 1936 Robert and Alice O'Grady deeded the Argyle property to Argyle Hotel Inc.,[39] which took out a mortgage for $16,000 from the American National Insurance Company. By May 1940 the O'Gradys were facing foreclosure of the mortgage. In an article headlined "Alamo Heights Inn Foreclosure Threatens," the *San Antonio Light* described the Argyle as "a hotel in name" yet "at once an institution, a history book of San Antonio, and a museum." The article continued:

> In danger of being foreclosed . . . the house still seems to echo with the tramp of Robert E. Lee . . . the voice of General John J. Pershing, and the anti-secession arguments of "Colonel" Charles Anderson . . . and the rhythmic voice of Hiram H. McLane . . . reciting his own blank verse poetry about the fall of the Alamo.[40]

After describing the history of the hotel beginning with Patterson's acquisition of the property from McLane, the article noted that the O'Gradys moved into the Argyle on Saint Patrick's Day in 1893 "and haven't moved out since." After serving as mayor continuously since 1922, Mr. Bob apparently entertained the idea of avoiding foreclosure by selling the Argyle to the city of Alamo Heights to be used as a library and recreation center,[41] a suggestion that was rejected. A year later, on May 23, 1941, the O'Gradys conveyed the Argyle to the holder of the mortgage, American National Insurance Company, in lieu of foreclosure. Thus ended the forty-eight-year O'Grady era. Unlike in previous decades, the senior military men gathered at Fort Sam Houston during World War II would not be able to repair to the Argyle for a fine meal and after-dinner snifter of brandy.

For several years after the O'Gradys' ownership of the Argyle came to an end, the building and grounds were evidently vacant, falling into a sad state of neglect and disrepair. Finally, in May 1944, the insurance company sold the property to Lucy W. White, who for the next eleven years operated it as a boardinghouse. During that period the Argyle changed hands three more times, though it continued to function as a poorly maintained, cheap boardinghouse. By 1955, Mr. Bob and Miss Alice O'Grady had long since passed away and the beautiful old inn at the top of Arsenal Hill, a "monument to history and to good living and good taste" in the words of Miss Alice, was facing a highly uncertain fate, including the possibility of demolition.

5

The Argyle Reborn

In 1941, Thomas Baker Slick was a young man in a hurry, with an audacious vision and the great wealth required to make the vision a reality. Slick was the oldest of three children of the late Tom Slick of Oklahoma City, known as the "King of the Wildcatters," who at the time of his death in 1930 was the largest independent oil operator in the United States. Young Tom, born in 1916, had been educated following his father's untimely death at the Phillips Exeter Academy in New Hampshire and then at Yale, where he graduated Phi Beta Kappa in 1938 with a degree in science. By the time of Tom's college graduation his mother, Berenice, and her second husband, Charles Urschel, had moved from Oklahoma City to San Antonio, where Berenice's sister Ramona resided with her husband, the prominent lawyer and judge Arthur Seeligson. Thus the young Tom Slick found his way to San Antonio, and it is fair to say that with his arrival the city was never quite the same again.

Unlike most young men who have inherited great wealth, Tom Slick was not only smart and well educated but impelled by a burning ambition; in his case, not so much to enlarge his wealth and possessions as to use them for the betterment of humankind, specifically by funding advances in scientific research that could change the world. In 1940 Slick purchased a number of contiguous ranches approximately eight miles west of downtown San Antonio, totaling some five thousand acres. Slick envisioned a portion of the property as the future campus of one or more scientific research institutions he intended to found; hence he named his ranch the Essar (as in *S* for science and *R* for research). In December 1941, just weeks after Pearl Harbor, Slick, at the age of twenty-five, signed the papers establishing the Foundation of Applied Research as an irrevocable charitable trust devoted to basic scientific research, to which he

Tom Slick (*right*) in 1941. (TBRI)

conveyed 1,600 acres and an interest in his oil and gas properties valued at $500,000.

The war years intervened, putting Slick's audacious vision on hold as he served on the War Production Board in Washington, DC, and later as an officer in the navy in the Pacific. At the end of the war he returned to San Antonio and immediately set about gearing up his new research institution. Having been educated at Exeter and Yale, Slick must have been painfully aware of the shortcomings of San Antonio in contrast to the great learning centers of the Northeast. Not only did San Antonio lack a research university, medical school, and teaching hospital in the 1940s, but its only educational institution that offered a degree more advanced than a bachelor's was St. Mary's University law school. In the aftermath of World War II the National Institutes of Health was in its infancy and only beginning to provide grants to investigators for medical research. Almost all medical research was conducted at medical schools, research universities, and a handful of private independent research institutes on the East and West Coasts, including the Cold Spring Harbor Laboratory in New York, the Jackson Laboratory in Maine, and the Scripps Research Institute in California.

The task of recruiting research scientists to Slick's fledgling Foundation of Applied Research (FAR)[1] in out-of-the-way San Antonio would be a formidable one; many must have scoffed at it as ridiculous. In the very beginning, during the war years, Slick was guided by a scientist named Dr. Gregory Pincus at the Worcester Foundation for Experimental Biology in Massachusetts. It is unclear how

Slick was acquainted with Dr. Pincus, but it may have been the result of Slick's interest in cattle breeding, particularly in the revolutionary science of artificial insemination for breeding superior livestock. Pincus was the first scientist to successfully experiment with in vitro fertilization of mammals in the 1930s and later pioneered oral contraception; by 1944 he was leading Tom Slick's effort to recruit scientists to his research venture in Texas.[2]

In the immediate postwar period there was a proliferation of private industrial research in the United States thanks to the many advances in industrial technology the war effort and defense budget had spawned. One such institution was the Midwest Research Institute in Kansas City, which had been founded a few years earlier to experiment with converting ammonium nitrate produced for military ordnance into agricultural fertilizer. The president of Midwest Research was Dr. Harold Vagtborg, who became intrigued with Tom Slick after reading an article in the *Kansas City Times* about the young oilman's dream to establish "a center where outstanding scientists will gather for experiments in animal husbandry, biology and chemistry" in order "to develop a research foundation for public service."[3] After corresponding with Slick, Vagtborg visited San Antonio in 1947 and persuaded Slick that in addition to the basic research mission envisioned for the FAR, he should establish a sister organization that would, like Midwest Research, conduct engineering research for the advancement of industrial technology. Thus in September 1947 Slick created the Southwest Research Institute as a second irrevocable charitable trust. Both organizations were located at

Tom Slick with his brother Earl at Cable House. (TBRI)

the Essar Ranch, with shared administrative offices in the renovated Cable House, a large Victorian home built in the nineteenth century by a Chicago railroad magnate named R. R. Cable. In 1948 Vagtborg accepted Slick's offer to head both the FAR and Southwest Research Institute.

From the very beginning, Tom Slick was preoccupied with the problem of attracting sufficient financial resources to support basic research at the FAR. But he was convinced that Southwest Research Institute could operate profitably within several years by contracting with industry and the government, and that its excess profits could provide a perpetual endowment to support basic research at the FAR. From the outset Slick sought to diversify the financial support for his nonprofit research institutes[4] so that they would not be dependent on the generosity of a single benefactor.

Despite his efforts, the FAR and Southwest Research Institute remained heavily dependent on Slick's contributions of capital, which by 1950 exceeded $2 million. The organizations' boards formed a development committee charged with seeking donations broadly in the community, but the committee's first report, for the period 1950–51, noted that almost two-thirds of the funds raised came from Tom Slick and his mother and brother. Though by 1953 Southwest Research Institute was thriving and operating in the black, it was still not in a position to provide financial support to its sister research institute, which was now known as the Southwest Foundation for Research and Education. Meanwhile, the latter's research mission had shifted away from an agricultural focus to a biomedical one. By then Congress had significantly increased the budget of the National Institutes of Health, and Southwest Foundation was repositioned to compete for federal grants supporting basic medical research in cancer, heart disease, polio, and reproductive medicine. In early 1955, Tom Slick's sister Betty hit on a brilliant if highly unconventional idea for a way to provide badly needed financial support for his struggling medical research institution. Betty had also moved to San Antonio from Oklahoma City with her husband, Lewis Moorman, shortly after World War II. Educated at Madeira School and Smith College, Betty was sophisticated and charming and by 1955 had been fully accepted into San Antonio's old social order. Harold Vagtborg recalled that in early 1955 he was invited to tea at Betty's home to meet with a small group of ladies to talk with them about the work being done by Southwest Foundation, which Vagtborg hoped would lead to the establishment of a women's auxiliary to support the Foundation.[5]

Three of the ladies at the tea, Betty Moorman, Margaret "Mag" Tobin, and Carolyn Negley, joined the Foundation's Board of Trustees. Betty then conceived the idea of starting "a social club of high caliber, with members obligated to make an annual contribution to the Foundation."[6] Well aware that the Argyle had fallen on hard times and had been reduced to a dilapidated boardinghouse, Betty suggested buying the property and then converting it into a private club whose members would fund the renovation of the building and grounds and make annual donations to the Foundation. It was a truly ingenious scheme, but like her brother Tom's dream of building a world-class research institution in sleepy South Texas, it was also truly audacious.

Tom Slick in a laboratory at the Southwest Foundation for Research and Education in the 1950s. (TBRI)

Betty Moorman was convinced the club concept could work if they could restore the Argyle to its former glory and win the support of the leading citizens in town, many of whom were already supporters of Tom Slick's research center.

Tom Slick embraced the concept, as did Betty's husband, Lew, and in the spring of 1955 they negotiated the purchase of the Argyle and finalized the structure for its conversion to a private club to support Southwest Foundation. This was detailed in a letter dated May 2, 1955, to Harold Vagtborg from Ed Gesick, treasurer of Southwest Foundation. Gesick wrote:

> Our women Trustees [Betty Moorman, Mag Tobin, and Carolyn Negley] have a project. Acting through Mary Chris Grant, Lew Moorman's sister, and with the tremendous enthusiasm of Betty Moorman, the old Argyle Hotel, a historic San Antonio landmark near the Olmos Dam, has been purchased for $32,500. Betty put up half of the money and Tom put up the other half, both of which will become loans to the Foundation, which will own the property. . . .
>
> The mechanics of the entire operation have not been worked out in detail but the general outline is as follows:
>
> A club will be formed on the lines of the Bayou Club in Houston to which members will be invited to join providing they make a $500 initial contribution to the Foundation plus a relatively small amount for annual dues. It is estimated that 200 memberships will be easily obtained. (Mesdames Tobin and Negley have been in on this all the way and feel that there will be no difficulty

> in having this number of memberships. . . .) Proceeds from these contributions will be used to rehabilitate the Argyle. . . . The third floor of the Argyle will have small suites set up for visiting scientists and other visitors.
>
> . . . Betty has tremendous enthusiasm for this project, the manager of which will be Lew Moorman's sister. Mesdames Tobin and Carolyn Negley are equally enthusiastic.

The plan was fully embraced by the board of Southwest Foundation from the outset. At a meeting of the Foundation's Executive Committee on May 24, 1955, Ed Gesick provided a full report on the plans for the acquisition of the Argyle Hotel and its conversion to a private club. According to the minutes of the meeting:

> Briefly, funds would be made available by loan or gift to the Foundation to acquire the property. The Argyle would then be restored and operated by the women Trustees or wives of Trustees through means of a club form of organization. The Foundation would receive funds, by means of contributions from club members, to restore the Argyle. The Argyle would become an in-town meeting place for visiting scientists, staff scientists, sponsors and Trustees. The Foundation would expect to receive rent, based on its investment, and yearly support from the Club members for Biomedical Research.

On May 25, 1955, Charles Haeuser, who then owned the Argyle,[7] sold the land and buildings (block 26, 1.2587 acres) to Mary Moorman Grant, trustee, for the cash price of $32,200. Mary "Chris" Grant was Lew Moorman's older sister and was acting as the representative for the real buyers, Tom Slick and Betty Moorman. From the beginning Betty Moorman had the active support of some of the city's most prominent women, who in addition to Mag Tobin and Carolyn Negley included her mother, Berenice Urschel, and aunt, Ramona Seeligson.[8] As Vagtborg noted, "with women like these behind the club, it was bound to succeed."[9] Even before the purchase of the property closed, Tom Slick and his sister Betty were seeking a variance from Alamo Heights zoning restrictions that would have precluded its use as a private club. Notwithstanding the opposition of a number of nearby property owners, the variance was granted by the city of Alamo Heights in June 1955, and the club's founders immediately moved forward to organize the club, solicit memberships, and finalize plans for the restoration of the building and grounds. The club would be overseen by a Board of Governors, three of whom would be appointed by the board of Southwest Foundation. The initial Board of Governors consisted of Betty Moorman, Tom Slick, Berenice Urschel, Harold Vagtborg, Mag Tobin, Carolyn Negley, Mrs. Frank Huntress, Robert Barclay, Mrs. John Bennett, Gilbert Denman, Hal Dewar, Bill Rhame, Jesse Oppenheimer, Mrs. Dale Dorn, and H. B. Zachry. The club's manager would be Chris Moorman Grant.

As Gesick correctly noted, the plan was to transfer ownership of the land and building to Southwest Foundation, which would then lease the building back to the Argyle Club, a newly formed entity. As the club's members would

The Argyle in 1955. (TBRI)

be required to make annual cash contributions to Southwest Foundation, the novel structure was intended to qualify for an income tax exemption, which tax attorney Jesse Oppenheimer was retained to seek from the IRS.[10] In July 1955 the organizers unveiled their plans for the new Argyle Club. Under the headline "Quaint Old Argyle Hotel Restoration Project Set," the *San Antonio Express* reported:

> The Argyle is now owned by the Southwest Foundation for Research and Education. The building will be leased to a club to be called the Argyle . . . [which] will have the dual role of a gathering place for scientists and other visitors to the foundation and for a dinner club. . . . Membership will be . . . at a cost of $500 plus an annual contribution of $100. After cost of restoring the Argyle is paid, the money thus paid in will go entirely for medical research.[11]

By September Betty and her team of go-getters were busy soliciting members from the city's social elite. Invitations to join were extended to six hundred couples or individuals, three hundred of whom had accepted by the end of the year. Each new member was required to pay a $500 initiation fee into a building fund, which was more than adequate to defray the cost of renovating the building and grounds and the club's interior decor. The club's organizers decided that the theme for the club's interior would be "Texas Under Six Flags," which was highly appropriate given the building's history.[12] Rather than select a single interior designer for the project, they enlisted a group of

Portrait of Betty Slick Moorman by the famous artist Madame Elizabeth Shoumatoff, best known for her *Unfinished Portrait of Franklin Roosevelt*. (Photo of painting owned by TBRI)

local interior decorators and one from out of state. The designer team consisted of San Antonio decorators Mildred English, Montgomery Cameron, Cornelia Gates, Eleanor Taylor, Bob Winn, Robert Sheffield, and Oklahoma City decorator Warren Ramsey, who had worked previously with the Slick and Urschel families. Different dining rooms and public areas of the club were dedicated to the six eras of Texas's rule.[13] For example, the dining room to the right of the entrance on the building's second floor was designated the French Room, and the dining suite to the left was the Spanish Room. The task of selecting the decor and furnishings for these period rooms and spaces was divided up among the interior decorators, which undoubtedly created challenges. Nationally prominent Joe Lambert from Dallas was selected for the landscape design, and the architects chosen for the renovation of the building were John R. Walker and O'Neil Ford.

Many of the original furnishings and art works were donated by its organizers and first members. These included Currier and Ives horse racing prints that had hung in the bar at the old Nimitz Hotel in Fredericksburg and two bronze steer heads that had originally adorned the entrance gates of the Chicago stockyards. The boar's head on a shield mounted on the wall of the Tap Room (today the bar), which became the club's logo, was crafted by Mrs. F. C. Hixon based on the crest of the Duke of Argyll. The Tap Room was designed to represent the Confederate era of Texas history, serving mint juleps in silver julep cups donated by Mag Tobin. It is unclear which period in Texas history the Hunt Room was designed to represent, as the large wooden

Currier and Ives print from the Nimitz Hotel. (Photo of print owned by TBRI)

Bronze steer heads from the Chicago stockyards. (Photo owned by TBRI)

wall hangings installed there were gifts from the Kreindler brothers, owners of the 21 Club in New York, who were friends of Betty and Lew Moorman. The wall hangings (many of which hang in the bar at 21 today) all celebrated the pleasures (and perils) of drinking, as they dated from 21's days as a renowned speakeasy during Prohibition.

By the spring of 1956 the renovation and interior decorations were nearing completion and plans were being made for a grand opening. Under the headline "Gala Opening Set for Famed Hotel," the *San Antonio Express* reported:

> The historic old Argyle Hotel—world renowned for its fine cuisine and gracious hospitality—is rapidly being restored to its former elegance and readied for a gala "Texas Under Six Flags" opening. . . . Decorators . . . are vying with each other to turn out the most beautiful rooms. . . . Antiques in keeping with the various periods are being collected from over the country. Some of the beautiful old antiques from the Argyle's early days have been retained.
>
> All proceeds from the Argyle will be used to help support medical research on cancer, leukemia, heart disease and hardening of the arteries now underway at the Southwest Foundation for Research and Education.[14]

The *San Antonio Light* reported that "the Argyle, fabulous in its day, is slated for an even more fabulous future as renovation nears completion. . . . [The club] will have a large main dining room and a tap room as well as several small dining rooms . . . [and] drawing rooms, meeting rooms and a recreation room."[15] Following a preopening event during Fiesta, the week-long celebration in San Antonio in the last week of April commemorating Texas independence, the beautifully renovated, furnished, and landscaped Argyle made its debut on May 26, 1956, amid considerable fanfare. Under the banner headline "Argyle a Veritable Jaunt through Texas' Past," the *San Antonio Light* reported that "at the old Argyle Hotel, reopened as a private club for supporters of Southwest Foundation for Research and Education, ghosts of many pasts echo through the walls." The Spanish Room is "filled with heavy, dark carved furniture against soft yellow-green walls and draperies," while "just across the hall you can step into a bit of France . . . with its pale gray walls, heavy white drapes, crystal chandelier . . . a pair of petit-point covered gold and white chairs and a round walnut table from New Orleans." In the downstairs bar and dining rooms "the informal frontier days of the Texas Republic are re-created on the white painted stone walls . . . [with] some of the original furnishings and accent pieces" and "a set of colored etchings depicting ancient Rio Grande river scenes." The article concluded by observing that "Mrs. Lewis Moorman was the general chairman for the refurnishing of the club" and that "Mrs. George Grant will be hostess."[16] The grand opening of the Argyle was widely reported in newspapers throughout the region, including the *Austin American-Statesman* and the *Daily Oklahoman*, which noted that "Joe Lambert of Dallas, famous throughout the southwest as a landscape artist, has designed the landscaping of the grounds to make a perfect setting for the big pale yellow frame building with its white columns and green shutters."[17]

From the beginning, the reborn Argyle fulfilled the dual objectives envisioned by Betty Moorman: providing vitally needed funding for basic medical research by Southwest Foundation and an elegant dining experience for members and their guests through the preservation and restoration of one of the great houses of Texas. The uniqueness of the Argyle's dual mission resulted in an Associated Press wire story in the fall of 1957 that was reproduced in newspapers across the nation. Under headlines such as "Swank Texas Club Pushes Science Cause," "Rich Texas Group Aids Scientists," and "Mink-and-Millions Texans Back Scientific Research" (to quote only a few), newspapers throughout the country[18] reported:

> Down here in one of America's oldest cities, the mink-and-millions set has a radical outlook—that basic scientific research should be supported financially for cultural reasons, just like the opera and symphony orchestra. And from this outlook stems one of the nation's exclusive clubs—the Argyle. The clubrooms themselves are fantastic. The members took over a century-old building that during its early days was a noted restaurant, a ranch-house and a hotel. The women of the club renovated it. They begged and borrowed antiques from across the South.[19]

In short order the Argyle acquired a reputation as one of the state's most exclusive clubs whose members were drawn not

Boar's head crest in the Argyle bar. (Photo owned by TBRI)

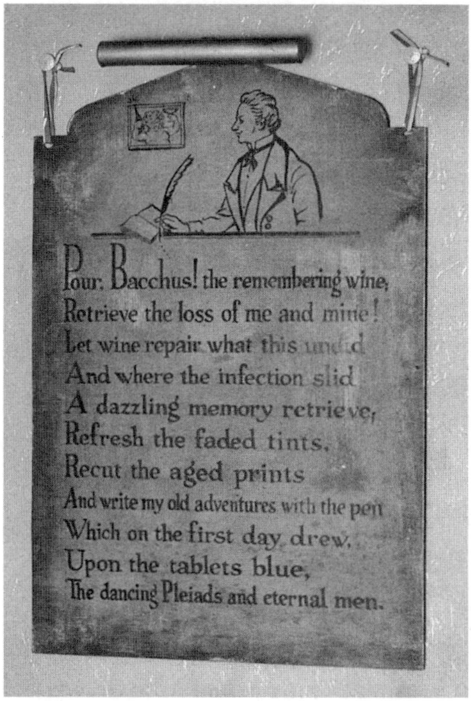

Wooden wall hanging in the Argyle Hunt Room. (Photo owned by TBRI)

only from San Antonio's social elite but from throughout the state and beyond. It captured the attention of the *New York Times,* which described it as "an exclusive social club [that] draws its members from all parts of the United States [and whose] social activities are secondary to its main purpose of contributing to scientific research."[20] Another Betty Moorman touch was the choice of a menu more in keeping with the 21 Club in New York than with Miss Alice's Old South. An early menu featured, for example, jellied madrilene with sour cream and red caviar, Argyle chicken crepes, shad roe wrapped in bacon, peppered bomb steak, and, like 21, a hamburger served with potato puffs and, with a nod to the memory of "Old George" Bannister, Argyle oyster stew. The menu also included a brief history of the Argyle, which perpetuated a number of notable inaccuracies, stating that it "epitomized the pleasant ways and good living of the storied South" and "was purchased in 1884 by two Scotsmen" before coming into the hands of "the fabulous Miss Alice O'Grady around the turn of the century." Commemorating the state's colorful history and preserving the building's storied past, with its thick limestone walls, cypress floors, and exposed piping, the Argyle quickly established a special ambience and charm that endures to this day.

By the time the Argyle opened as an elegant dining club in 1956, the biomedical research programs at Southwest Foundation were becoming more robust in several areas of focus. Possibly because of the continuing influence of the Worcester Foundation's Dr. Pincus, a pioneer in artificial insemination, as a scientific adviser to Tom Slick, by the mid-1950s Southwest Foundation was conducting extensive research in human reproductive science under the leadership of Dr. Joseph Goldzieher. Goldzieher led a team that over the next fifteen years played an important role in the development and testing of the first oral contraceptive—the "pill."[21] In 1958 the discovery that baboons could naturally develop atherosclerosis led to the establishment of a nonhuman primate colony that would eventually become one of the largest in the world.[22] Although chimpanzees had been used extensively in the development of the polio vaccine, prior to 1960 there had been little use of nonhuman primates as laboratory animal models for the study of human disease. Recognizing the potential of baboons for the study of atherosclerosis (and the relative ease of work-

12-D SAN ANTONIO LIGHT Sunday, May [illegible]

Argyle a Veritable Jaunt Through Texas' Past

A SPANISH GOVERNOR WOULD FEEL AT HOME HERE
Oak, red velvet, iron all from another era.

TIME HANGS HEAVY OVER THY HEAD
An iron chandelier in clock form.

THE FIREPLACE IN THE TAVERN ROOM AT THE ARGYLE
Boar's head is symbolic theme of early era.

FRENCH INFLUENCE REFLECTED IN LADIES' CARD ROOM
Pale grey and white touched with gold is theme.

All Government Eras Represented

By JEANNE BARNES

Every era of government in Texas left its mark architecturally and in furnishings for homes as well as in the name places and the descendants themselves.

But seldom have all the different ways of life been collected all under one roof so that by walking from one room to another, a picture of the past opens up before you.

Such a picture is unfolding for the first time in San Antonio. At the old Argyle Hotel, reopened as a private club for supporters of Southwest Foundation for Research and Education, ghosts of many pasts echo through the walls.

There's the Spanish suite, where grandees and governors and their ladies would feel at home. It's filled with heavy, dark carved oak furniture against soft yellow-green walls and draperies. Deep red velvet upholstery and orange-red Oriental rugs on the floors provide accent.

* * *

The suite includes a sitting

... all the accessories are in keeping.

Floors of the upstairs are particularly gay, painted black, dark green or white with pink flowers and gold hearts and stars splattered on them.

* * *

On the first floor, the informal frontier days of the Texas Republic are re-created in the white-painted stone walls, the round and square pine tables, some out of the original furnishings and the recent pieces.

Currier and Ives prints of horse racing scenes which hung in the Old Nimitz Hotel bar in Fredericksburg around the time of the Civil war and a set of colored etchings depicting ancient Rio Grande river scenes are real museum pieces.

The latter group include scenes at Wild Rose Pass, Frontera, Las Isletas, the falls of Presidio and Rio San Pedro.

A pair of bronzed steer heads which once marked the gates of the Chicago stockyards and a ceramic boar's

Barbecue Dinner for Daughters

Mrs. John S. Hammonds will entertain the Barnard E. Bee chapter, UDC, with a barbecue dinner June 5 at her home on Pipe Creek, honoring the new and retiring officers.

Mrs. Robert Beath will install the following new officers: Mesdames Fred Mooty, president; A. I. Kliefoth, Frank Naeglin and Cordia Bales, vice presidents; R. U. Akins, treasurer; R. C. Gatlin, secretary; Edith Thacker, corresponding secretary and publicity chairman; A. A. Szafranski, registrar; M. H. Hewett, historian; George Surkey, custodian, and Robert Beach, recorder of crosses.

Incarnate Word

Japanese garden sunback

San Antonio Light, May 27, 1956.

ing with baboons relative to other large apes), Southwest Foundation established a facility in Kenya in 1958 to capture wild baboons and ship them to San Antonio. By the 1960s these had grown to a large colony, the use of which rapidly expanded beyond the study of coronary artery disease to a host of other common chronic human diseases.

Tragically, Tom Slick did not live to see his research institutions reach the national and international prominence they ultimately attained; he died in the crash of a small plane in 1962 en route home to San Antonio from a trip to the West Coast. Along with the Argyle, Southwest Foundation, Southwest Research Institute, and the Mind Science Foundation survived this loss thanks largely to major bequests from Tom Slick's estate and generous gifts from his mother, Berenice, and brother Earl. During the formative years of the late 1950s and early 1960s the Argyle continued to be managed by Chris Grant, who lived in the building with her husband and high school–aged children. Chris was an artist and gracious hostess with a sure understanding of the intentions and wishes of the club's founders and early membership.

In 1965 the club's Board of Governors decided to hire a professional manager and offered the position to a young Denver native named Mel Weingart who was then managing one of Dallas's downtown dining clubs. Though his greatest aspiration was to be an opera singer, Mel had a college degree in hotel and restaurant management. Over the succeeding decades the Argyle would acquire a reputation for its excellent cuisine, but in the 1960s, rather than a chef, the club had a cook named Charles Murray whose previous culinary experience had been in cramped kitchens on board trains on the Southern Pacific railroad. To his dismay Weingart discovered that the only wine served by the club consisted of cheap jug wine such as Mateus and Lancer's. Rather than replace the staff, Mel set about methodically training them in the culinary arts, each day personally tasting and adjusting each entrée and sauce before lunch and dinner and being as much a presence in the kitchen as in the front of the "house" visiting with members. At a time when Americans were only beginning to appreciate (and to produce) good wine, he began to build an excellent wine cellar.

In the years following Weingart's arrival the club grew significantly, and by 1969 there was a long waiting list of applicants for admission. In that year, however, Mel was offered the opportunity to pursue his first love, a career with the Metropolitan Opera in New York. With his wife, Sandy, and two young sons, he decamped for Manhattan, where for the next three years he sang in the opera and lived with his family in the Park Avenue townhouse that belonged to the eccentric San Antonio art collector and patron of the opera Robert Tobin. During Weingart's absence the Argyle's affairs quickly began to deteriorate. In 1972 Betty and Lew Moorman persuaded him to give up his opera career and return to San Antonio to manage the club. In short order he was able to put the Argyle's house back in order and during the 1970s carefully honed the club's reputation for impeccable service and superb cuisine in an atmosphere of understated elegance with a strong suggestion of Southern hospitality.

By the mid-1980s the number of resident members was capped at 825, with several hundred more nonresident members, all of whom were required to make an annual donation of $500 to Southwest Foundation, generating over half a million dollars annually to augment the Foundation's endowment. With a long waiting list for admission, the Argyle had acquired a unique reputation that extended far beyond San Antonio. An article that appeared in a 1986 issue of *Texas Monthly* described a luncheon hosted by B. A. Bentsen, the wife of Texas senator Lloyd Bentsen, for Nancy Reagan in Washington, DC:

> Like hundreds of well-bred South Texans before her, the senator's wife had turned to San Antonio's select Argyle Club—and to Weingart, its long-time manager and arbiter extraordinaire—when things had to be, well, perfect. Weingart could be trusted to take care of everything in that ever-so-comfortable but unmistakably upper class Argyle style. . . . For 127 years . . . the pillared, deep-verandahed building that is the Argyle Club has been an exemplar of the style by which San Antonio identifies itself. And for much of that time, it has been an exemplar of something larger—the civilizing impulse at work.[23]

The Argyle's "civilizing impulse" under Mel Weingart's management can be traced directly back to its origins under haughty Charles Anderson, erudite Hiram McLane, charming Miss Alice O'Grady, and the sophisticated likes of Betty Moorman, Mag Tobin, and Caroline Negley. Although the

Argyle epitomizes fine dining in elegant surroundings (a dress code is strictly enforced), it also captures the unique ranching ethos of South Texas. Thus during the dove and quail hunting seasons members are permitted to dine in their casual hunting outfits in the Hunt Room, bringing their bagged game with them if they choose, which is then picked by the kitchen staff and served to order. Chicken-fried quail remains a popular entrée.

Mel Weingart at the Argyle in 1986. (Photo by Robert Maxham)

6

The Argyle Today

Judged from the outside, the Argyle today has a timeless quality, the graceful, pale yellow Southern mansion with its broad portico and thick pillars, set back on a wide lawn with live oaks and magnolias, seemingly unchanged in the sixty years since its rebirth as a private club. While over the decades there have been subtle changes to the club's interior decor and several additions (notably the Coates dining area and the Slick-Urschel room for large groups and parties), the essential ambience of the Argyle, owing to the eclectic assortment of antiques, artwork, flooring, exposed piping, and paint colors, has remained faithfully intact. The dedication to fine dining in elegant surroundings has also been carefully maintained thanks to the stewardship of the club's managers and the oversight of its Board of Governors. Memories of the original Texas under Six Flags theme of the club gradually faded, though members still refer to the French and Spanish Rooms upstairs without understanding why they are so named. But the central purpose of the club—to provide a perpetual, living endowment for basic scientific research—has not only endured but increased in importance. Each resident member today is required to make an annual contribution of $1,000 to the Texas Biomedical Research Institute (as Southwest Foundation was renamed in 2012), generating approximately $1.2 million in unrestricted cash each year to support the institute's research budget. An annual gala hosted at the Argyle by the institute's women's support group, the Forum, generates another $300,000 to $400,000. Institute researchers regularly give talks to large lay audiences at Argyle luncheons hosted by the Forum as well as at evening "Fireside Chats" open to all Argyle members. Another support group, the Founder's Council, organizes lectures by institute scientists for its members, whose donations support pilot research projects.

Today the Texas Biomedical Research Institute is one of the nation's leading independent private medical research institutes, with internationally recognized programs in virology, immunology, and genetics. By the 1980s its nonhuman primate colony had been expanded to include chimpanzees and a number of monkey species that are particularly useful in studying human infectious diseases and developing vaccines to block their transmission. The baboon colony was selectively bred over multiple generations to produce distinct pedigrees that offer a unique resource for the study of common and genetically influenced diseases. In addition to the pioneering work in coronary artery disease, the baboon colony has provided unique resources for the study of human fetal development, including lifesaving interventions for prematurely born infants. In the 1990s the colony was designated by the National Institutes of Health as the

Southwest National Primate Research Center, one of the nation's seven regional primate research centers. Among major medical advances in which the institute's researchers have played an important part using the nonhuman primate resources are vaccines to prevent infection by the hepatitis B and C viruses, a high-speed ventilator for severely premature infants, antiviral drugs to treat HIV-AIDS, and understanding of the mechanisms and genetics of such common diseases as atherosclerosis, diabetes, obesity, osteoporosis, and epilepsy.

The primary focus of research at Texas Biomedical today is the threat to global human health from common infectious diseases ranging from HIV-AIDS, tuberculosis, malaria, and SARS to hemorrhagic fevers such as Ebola and bioterrorism threats such as anthrax and the Marburg virus.

The Texas Biomedical Research Institute. (TBRI)

Since 2000 Texas Biomedical has operated a Biosafety Level 4 laboratory, a maximum containment facility in which the world's most lethal pathogens can be studied, one of only four such labs in the United States and the only one that is privately owned. The combination of a BSL-4 lab with one of the NIH-designated regional primate research centers makes Texas Biomedical one of the unique research institutions in the world for the study of infectious diseases. Though small in comparison to major medical schools, the institute is home to researchers who have been highly successful in attracting federal and other research grants and contracts and have led internationally recognized research initiatives. For example, in 2015, the work of two of the institute's scientists was featured on the covers of *Science* and *Nature,* the most prestigious journals in medical research, for their work on Ebola and malaria. Thus the Argyle today has amply fulfilled the vision of its founders of providing a permanent endowment to support basic biomedical research while richly preserving the fascinating historical legacy of its years as a ranching headquarters, fine dining establishment, and overnight inn.

Notes

Chapter 1

1. Among the many great public spaces designed by Olmsted were Central Park in New York City and Golden Gate Park in San Francisco.

2. Clinton P. Hartmann, "Anderson, Charles," *Handbook of Texas Online*, Texas State Historical Association, June 9, 2010, http://tshaonline.org/handbook/online/articles/fan03.

3. David T. Dixon, *The Lost Gettysburg Address* (Santa Barbara, CA: B-List History, 2015), 16.

4. Ibid.

5. Ohio History Central, "Charles Anderson," accessed August 7, 2018, http://www.ohiohistorycentral.org/w/Charles_Anderson.

6. Ibid.

7. Dixon, *Lost Gettysburg Address*, 41.

8. Ibid., 53.

9. Ohio History Central, "Charles Anderson."

10. Frank W. Jennings, *San Antonio: The Story of an Enchanted City* (*San Antonio Express-News*, 1998), 70–71.

11. Ann Graham Gaines, "San Fernando Cathedral," *Handbook of Texas Online*, Texas State Historical Association, June 15, 2010, http://tshaonline.org/handbook/online/articles/ivs01.

12. The city was named for Saint Anthony of Padua.

13. In 1836 the newly arrived settlers declared their independence from Mexico and, after the fall of the Alamo, decisively defeated the Mexican army commanded by General Santa Anna at the Battle of San Jacinto in April 1836. Texas thereupon became an independent sover-

eign nation recognized by the governments of the United States and the principal European powers.

14. Jennings, *San Antonio,* 121.

15. Eldon Cagle, *Fort Sam Houston* (San Antonio: Maverick, 2003), 3.

16. Ibid., 4.

17. Kathryn Carter, *Stagecoach Inns of Texas* (Waco, TX: Texian Press, 1972), 24.

18. Jennings, *San Antonio,* 37; Dick McCracken, "Avoca, Texas" (Irish Cultural Society of San Antonio, October 2000).

19. On October 5, 2000, a building named for Avoca was dedicated on the campus of the Catholic University of the Incarnate Word, which is located on the site of the ghost township. Four of the nuns attending the ceremony were Irish immigrants.

20. Carter, *Stagecoach Inns of Texas,* 24.

21. Alice O'Grady, *The Argyle Cookbook* (San Antonio: Naylor, 1940), xiii.

22. Johnston, whose antebellum plantation "China Grove" was south of Houston, later served as a general in the Confederate Army in command of the Western Military Department, encompassing the entire area west of the Allegheny Mountains. He was killed in the Battle of Shiloh and buried in the Texas State Cemetery in Austin.

23. Cagle, *Fort Sam Houston,* 5.

24. Robert E. Lee Jr., *Recollections and Letters of General Robert E. Lee* (Garden City, NY: Garden City Publishing, 1904), 23.

25. Dixon, *Lost Gettysburg Address,* 67.

26. Ibid., 62.

27. The Knights of the Golden Circle was a secret society originally organized to push for the colonization of territory in northern Mexico by slave-owning Americans. It evolved into a pro-Confederate militia after the outbreak of the Civil War. James M. McPherson, *The Battle Cry of Freedom* (Oxford: Oxford University Press, 1988), 116.

28. Frank W. Jennings, "The Argyle's Fascinating History," *Journal of the Life and Culture of San Antonio,* University of the Incarnate Word, accessed August 7, 2018, www.uiw.edu/sanantonio/jenningsargyle.html.

29. Cagle, *Fort Sam Houston,* 5.

30. Marquis James, *The Raven* (New York: Macmillan, 1929), 410.

31. Michael Korda, *Clouds of Glory* (New York: Harper, 2014), 221.

32. Cagle, *Fort Sam Houston*, 9.

33. Korda, *Clouds of Glory*, 223.

34. The deed, signed by Charles and Eliza Anderson, was dated September 26, 1861.

35. Dixon, *Lost Gettysburg Address*, 76.

36. Ibid., 78–79.

37. Today this is the site of the corporate headquarters of the H. E. Butt Grocery Company.

38. Dixon, *Lost Gettysburg Address*, 83.

39. Ibid., 93–98.

40. Ibid., 103.

41. The Tredegar Iron Works in Richmond, Virginia, the largest of its kind in the South, supplied vital munitions to the Confederate Army. It is estimated that Virginia and North Carolina supplied a larger number of troops to the Confederate Army than any other state (Randolph H. McKim, *The Numerical Strength of the Confederate Army*, New York: Neale Publishing, 1912), and North Carolina provisioned the Army of Northern Virginia with critical supplies of flour and bacon.

42. Korda, *Clouds of Glory*, 226.

Chapter 2

1. Dixon, *Lost Gettysburg Address*, 22.

2. John K. Ward, "The Man Who Surrendered Fort Sumter," *Military History* 14, no. 6 (February 1998): 34.

3. C. Vann Woodward, *Mary Chesnut's Civil War* (New Haven, CT: Yale University Press, 1981), 40.

4. Shelby Foote, *The Civil War: A Narrative*, vol. 1 (New York: Random House, 1958), 48.

5. Woodward, *Mary Chesnut's Civil War*, 45.

6. *Harper's New Monthly Magazine* 23 (June 1861): 120.

7. Ibid., 120–21.

8. Ibid.

9. Blair House today serves as the official residence of visiting heads of state.

10. Korda, *Clouds of Glory*, 228.

11. Douglas Southall Freeman, *Robert E. Lee: A Biography*, vol. 1 (New York: Scribner, 1934), 28n.

12. Lee, *Recollections and Letters*, 25.

13. Ibid., 26, 27.

14. When Lincoln was urged early in the war to emancipate the slaves in the border states, he is reputed to have protested that to do so would be to risk losing Kentucky to the Confederacy. The abolitionist responded that if he were to free the slaves, Lincoln "would have God on his side," to which Lincoln rejoined, "I hope to have God on my side, but I *must* have Kentucky." Aaron Astor, "Bluegrass Blues and Grays," *New York Times*, May 7, 2011.

15. David Herbert Donald, *Lincoln* (New York: Simon and Schuster, 1995), 300.

16. Foote, *Civil War*, vol. 1, 88.

17. Ibid.

18. Joshua F. Speed to Abraham Lincoln, October 7, 1861, Abraham Lincoln Papers, Library of Congress.

19. Foote, *Civil War*, vol. 1, 89.

20. Dixon, *Lost Gettysburg Address*, 108.

21. Ibid.

22. William G. Schmidt, "History of the 93rd Ohio Volunteer Infantry," http://myplace.frontier.com/~williamgschmidt/93rdovi/index.htm.

23. Shelby Foote, *The Civil War: A Narrative*, vol. 2 (New York: Random House, 1963), 82.

24. Ibid., 87.

25. This was also known as the Second Battle of Murfreesboro.

26. Foote, *Civil War*, vol. 2, 87–100.

27. "93rd Regiment Ohio Volunteer Infantry (1862–1865)," Ohio Civil War Central, 2016, https://www.ohiocivilwarcentral.com/entry.php?rec=1156.

28. A facsimile of the letter, dated either January 2 or January 7, 1863, is contained in "Ohio Regimental Files," National Park Service, accessed August 7, 2018, www.nps.gov/stri/learn/historyculture/regfohio.htm.

29. James McPherson, *Battle Cry of Freedom* (Oxford University Press, 1988), 596.

30. Ibid.

31. Ibid., 597.

32. Ibid., 598.

33. Ibid., 685.

34. Ibid., 686.

35. Osman C. Hooper, "John Brough," *Ohio Archaeological and Historical Publications*, 1904, 40–70.

36. Dixon, *Lost Gettysburg Address*, 156.

37. The discovery led David Dixon to write *The Lost Gettysburg Address*.

38. Dixon, *Lost Gettysburg Address*, 157.

39. Ibid., 158.

40. Ibid., 161.

41. Christopher Dickey, *Our Man in Charleston* (New York: Crown Publishers, 2015), 325.

42. Ibid., 34.

Chapter 3

1. Jennings, "Argyle's Fascinating History."

2. S. W. Pease and Crystal Sasse Ragsdale, "McLane, Hiram H.," *Handbook of Texas Online*, Texas State Historical Association, June 15, 2010, www.tshaonline.org/handbook/online/articles/fmc82.

3. For example, T. R. Fehrenbach made no mention of the expedition in his exhaustive history of Mexico, *Fire and Blood*.

4. Harris Gaylord Warren, "Gutierrez-Magee Expedition," *Handbook of Texas Online*, Texas State Historical Association, June 15, 2010, www.tshaonline.org/handbook/online/articles/qyg01.

5. Ibid.

6. Jennings, "Argyle's Fascinating History," 2.

7. Adolphe Giesecke Jr., "The Argyle Hotel," *Junior Historian* 11, no. 1 (September 1950): 27.

8. William McLane, "William McLane's Narrative of the Magee-Gutierrez Expedition, 1812–1813," edited by Henry P. Walker, *Southwestern Historical Quarterly* 66 (July 1962–April 1963): 569.

9. Giesecke, "Argyle Hotel," 27.

10. Hiram McLane, *The Capture of the Alamo* (San Antonio: San Antonio Printing, 1886), 8.

11. Ibid. 84.

12. Marilyn McAdams Sibley, *George W. Brackenridge: Maverick Philanthropist* (Austin: University of Texas Press, 1973), 22.

13. Ibid., 34.

14. Ibid., 47–48.

15. Ibid., 37.

16. Ibid., 80.

17. Brackenridge was the founder of the First National Bank of San Antonio and the majority owner of the *San Antonio Express* newspaper, among other business ventures. He was an original member of the Board of Regents of the University of Texas and its longest-serving member. When he died at the age of eighty-eight in 1920, he bequeathed his fortune to establish the George W. Brackenridge Foundation, which largely supports higher education.

18. Frederick Law Olmsted, *A Journey through Texas or a Saddle-Trip in the Southwestern Frontier* (New York: Dix, Edwards, 1857), 156–57.

19. Brackenridge, a lifelong champion of temperance, stipulated that no alcoholic beverages could be sold in the park.

20. Quoting from the deed recorded in the Bexar County Courthouse.

21. O'Grady, *Argyle Cookbook*, xiv.

Chapter 4

1. "Old Argyle Hotel's History Book of S.A.," *San Antonio Light*, May 19, 1940.

2. "O'Grady, John G.," *Handbook of Texas Online*, accessed August 7, 2018, www.tshaonline.org/handbook/online/articles/fog10.

3. "A Brief History of Boerne," *Hill Country Explore Magazine*, August 27, 2014, www.hillcountryexplore.com/?p=4175.

4. Ibid.

5. O'Grady, *Argyle Cookbook*, xiv.

6. "Brief History."

7. Ibid.

8. O'Grady, *Argyle Cookbook*, xiv.

9. Ibid., xi–xii.

10. This was originally the Kaiser Wilhelm district until the name was anglicized during World War I.

11. Cagle, *Fort Sam Houston*, 10.

12. Ibid., 22.

13. Ibid., 54.

14. Brian Dwyer, "Fort Sam Houston Revives Historic Structures for

BRAC Arrivals," US Army, April 3, 2009, www.army.mil/article/19252/fort_sam_houston_revives_historic_structures_for_BRAC_arrivals.

15. Jack McCallum, *Leonard Wood: Rough Rider, Surgeon, Architect of American Imperialism* (New York: New York University Press, 2006), 52–55.

16. Ibid., 63.

17. O'Grady, *Argyle Cookbook*, xvii.

18. Funston had been expected to command the American Expeditionary Force in France if the United States entered World War I but died of a massive heart attack in the lobby of the St. Anthony Hotel in San Antonio listening to the orchestra play the "Blue Danube" waltz. His body lay in state in the Alamo. *World Herald* (Omaha, NE), February 20, 1917; *Daily News* (Greensboro, NC), March 2, 1917.

19. Gene Smith, *Until the Last Trumpet Sounds: The Life of the General of the Armies John J. Pershing* (New York: John Wiley and Sons, 1998), 148–49.

20. O'Grady, *Argyle Cookbook*, xviii.

21. T. R. Fehrenbach, "Alamo Heights in Perspective," in *Golden Anniversary Alamo Heights Texas, 1922–1972* (Alamo Heights, TX: 1972).

22. M. H. Townsend obituary, *Weimar* (TX) *Mercury*, July 2, 1915.

23. Fehrenbach, "Alamo Heights in Perspective."

24. Quoting from the deed recorded at the Bexar County Courthouse.

25. Fehrenbach, "Alamo Heights in Perspective."

26. *Model T Journal*, no. 2007, Texas Transportation Museum. In the mid-1920s George sold the Ford dealership to Herpel-Gillespie to raise funds for the construction of the Medical Arts Building on Alamo Plaza, which today is the Emily Morgan Hotel.

27. Tom Walker, "The Autumn of Alamo Heights," *Texas Monthly*, May 1982.

28. *A Visitor's Guide to San Antonio* (San Antonio: Nic Tengg, 1913).

29. *San Antonio Historical and Modern; the City of Sunshine and Flowers* (privately printed, 1909).

30. *San Antonio Light*, September 16, 1941.

31. Jennings, "Argyle's Fascinating History," 2.

32. *San Antonio Light*, May 19, 1940.

33. Ibid.

34. Ella K. Daggett, "Famous Contemporaries: The Argyle and the Menger," *Southern Home and Garden*, September 1941.

35. Allyson Cook, "Icing on the Cake," *Texas Monthly*, January 1986.

36. *San Antonio Light*, May 19, 1940.

37. Jennings, "Argyle's Fascinating History," 3.

38. At the time of the accident, all of Ms. Mansfield's scenes had been filmed and the movie was released nationwide. She was one of Hollywood's leading actresses at the time of her death, having starred in *Dr. Jekyll and Mr. Hyde* opposite John Barrymore.

39. At some previous date Bob O'Grady had transferred an ownership interest in the Argyle to his sister Alice.

40. *San Antonio Light*, May 19, 1940.

41. Ibid.

Chapter 5

1. Slick made a poor choice in naming the institution, as it was not engaged in "applied" research nor was it a "foundation" in the usual sense. By the 1950s it was renamed the Southwest Foundation for Research and Education and today is the Texas Biomedical Research Institute.

2. Harold Vagtborg, *The Story of Southwest Research Center* (San Antonio: Southwest Research Institute, 1973), 20.

3. Ibid., 26–52.

4. A third organization, the Institute for Inventive Research, was formed by Slick in the 1940s but did not survive. In 1958 Slick founded the Mind Science Foundation to study parapsychology, which today conducts research on the mind.

5. Vagtborg, *Story of Southwest Research Center*, 355.

6. Ibid., 356.

7. The boardinghouse continued to be operated by Lucy Waters.

8. Mag Tobin was once described as "the grande dame nonpareil of Alamo Heights," who "when she's for you, she's with you all the way but when she's against you, you'd best get the hell out of the way." Walker, "Autumn of Alamo Heights."

9. Vagtborg, *Story of Southwest Research Center*, 357.

10. Both the Southwest Foundation for Research and Education

and the Southwest Research Institute were granted tax-exempt status; Slick's third research entity, the Institute for Inventive Research, failed to receive a tax exemption, which largely accounted for its demise.

11. *San Antonio Express*, July 10, 1955.

12. This was long before the creation of the theme parks of the same name.

13. Texas had been under the flags of France, Spain, Mexico, the Republic of Texas, the Confederacy, and the United States.

14. *San Antonio Express*, March 18, 1956.

15. *San Antonio Light*, May 27, 1956.

16. Ibid.

17. *Daily Oklahoman* (Oklahoma City, OK), May 27, 1956.

18. The papers included the *Raleigh (NC) Times*, the *Baltimore Sun*, the *New Rochelle (NY) Standard Star*, the *Santa Cruz (CA) Sentinel*, the *Sarasota (FL) Journal*, the *Toledo (OH) Blade*, the *Richmond (VA) News Leader*, the *Seattle Times*, and the *Detroit News*.

19. November 13, 1957, edition of the above-named newspapers.

20. *New York Times*, November 17, 1957.

21. Vagtborg, *Story of Southwest Research Center*, 359.

22. Ibid., 376

23. Cook, "Icing on the Cake."

Index

Alamo Heights, city of, 63, 64
Alamo Heights(subdivision); early development, 54, 58, 59; later development, 60–63; original plat, 49
Anderson, Charles; battle wound, 28–30; birth and early life, 4; building of house, 10; command of the 93rd Ohio Volunteer Infantry, 26–30; early political career, 4, 5; election as lieutenant governor of Ohio, 33–35; flight from Texas 14–16; governor of Ohio, 38; horse breeding operation, 8, 10; legal career in Ohio, 5; marriage, 4; move to San Antonio, 5; opposition to secession, 11, 12; special envoy to Great Britain, 26; speech at Gettysburg, 35–37; retirement and death, 38
Anderson, Robert; ceremonial flag-raising at Fort Sumter, 37; command of Fort Sumter, 18–20; command of Military Department of Kentucky, 25; education, 17; retirement from the army, 25, 26; service in Mexican-American War, 17
Argyle, The; as an overnight inn and dining establishment, 50, 53, 58, 61; under management of Miss Alice O'Grady; 53, 54, 56–58; Southern cuisine and ambiance, 64–68; conversion to private club, 78–89; support for biomedical research, 80, 83, 97, 98
Army of the Cumberland, 27
Arsenal Hill, 39
Avoca township, 8–10

baboon colony for research, 93
Battle of Rosilla, 40
Battle of Stones River, 27–29
Blair, Francis, 22, 23
Blue Hole, the, 47
Brackenridge, George W.; business career, 47; contraband cotton trade, 46, 47; construction of Fernridge, 47; creation of Brackenridge Park, 48; early life and education, 46; opposition to secession, 46; purchase of Alamo Heights property, 47
Bragg, Braxton, 27
Brough, John, 33–35
Bullis, John Lapham, 42, 58

Cable House, 76
Carr, Lucy Tobin, 50, 51
Chamberlain Investment Company, 52
Chesnut, Mary, 18, 19
Circle Dot Breed, 41

Fort Sam Houston; expansion, 55, 56; naming, 55; the Quadrangle, 54, 55
Fort Sumter; attack on, 17–19; consequences of capture by Confederates, 20–22
Foundation of Applied Research; baboon colony, 93; early focus of research programs, 91–93; ownership of Argyle property, 81; renamed, 77

George, Clifton; development of Alamo Heights subdivision, 60; Ford dealership, 60; invitation of President Taft to tea, 60
Gesick Ed, 80
Goldzieher, Dr. Joseph, 92
Grant, Mary Chris Moorman, 81, 88, 93
Gutiérrez-Magee Expedition, 39, 40

Herff, Ferdinand, 51
Houston, Sam, 12

Kentucky, neutrality in the Civil War, 25
Knights of the Golden Circle, 11, 12, 15

Lee, Robert E.; army service in Texas, 10, 11; confrontation with Texas secessionists, 13, 14; founder of St. Mark's church, 10, 11; friendship with Charles Anderson, 10, 14; meeting with Winfield Scott, 23, 24; opposition to secession, 12–14, 24; resignation of commission, 24
Lincoln, Abraham; call for volunteer troops, 20, 22; Military Department of Kentucky, 25

Mansfield, Martha, 66–68
McCulloch, Ben, 15
McLane, Hiram; horse breeding operation 41, 42; marriage and children, 41; move to Texas, 40;publication of novel *Irene Viesca*, 42; publication of *The Capture of the Alamo*, 42–44; sale of the Anderson property, 48; violin collection, 42
McLane, William; account of Gutiérrez-Magee Expedition, 42; participation in Gutiérrez-Magee Expedition, 40; purchase of Anderson home, 15, 41; death, 41
Menger Hotel, 11, 12
Mexican-American War, 5–7
Moorman, Betty Slick; conception of Argyle Club, 77, 78; education, 77; oversight of renovations and furnishings, 88; purchase of Argyle property, 80, 81; service on Board of Governors, 81; solicitation of members, 83
Moorman, Lewis, 77, 79, 87

Negley, Carolyn, 78, 79, 81

O'Grady, Alice; Argyle Cookbook,

53; early life, 52; entertaining senior army officers, 58; reopening of Argyle Hotel, 53; southern ambiance and cuisine, 64, 65
O'Grady, John G., 51
O'Grady, Robert; early life, 52; mayor of Alamo Heights, 64, 71; mortgage and foreclosure of hotel, 70, 71; purchase of Argyle Hotel, 59

Patterson, W. J. Ballantyne; additions to building, 50; failure of Alamo Heights subdivision, 59; hiring of O'Gradys to manage hotel, 52; opening of Argyle Hotel, 50; platting of Alamo Heights subdivision, 49; purchase of McLane property, 48
Pincus, Dr. Gregory, 74, 75, 91

Roosevelt, Theodore, 56
Rosecrans, William, 27, 28
Rough Riders, 56

San Antonio; early Spanish settlement, 5, 6; immigration from the South and from Germany, 6; impact of Mexican-American War, 6, 7
San Fernando Cathedral, 6
Secession crisis, 11–14, 16, 22
Seeligson, Arthur and Ramona, 72
Sisters of Charity of the Incarnate Word, 48
Slick, Thomas Baker; birth and education, 72; acquisition of Essar Ranch, 73; creation of the Foundation of Applied Research, 73; creation of Southwest Research Institute, 75, 76; financial support for the research institutes, 77; support for the Argyle club concept, 79; untimely death, 93; wartime service, 74
Southwest National Primate Research Center, 99
Speed, Joshua, 25
Surrender of Federal troops in Texas to Confederates, 13
Sweet, James R., 47

Texas Biomedical Research Institute, 98–100
The Alamo, 6
The Warrens of Virginia (film), 66–68
Tobin, Margaret "Mag," 78, 79, 81, 85
Townsend, Marcus Hervey, 59
Twiggs, David, 13

Urschel, Charles and Berenice, 72

Vagtborg, Dr. Harold; head of Midwest research Institute, 75; named president of FAR and Southwest Research Institute, 76; recruitment of Betty Moorman to support FAR, 77
Vallandigham, Clement; arrest and release, 32; campaign for Ohio governor, 31–35

Weingart, Mel; hired as club manager, 93; career with Metropolitan Opera, 94; reputation for fine dining, 94
White, Lucy, 71
Wood, Leonard, 56